When
HAPPINESS
IS NOT
ENOUGH

Balancing Pleasure and Achievement in Your Life

CHRIS SKELLETT

EXISLE
PUBLISHING

First published 2011

Exisle Publishing Pty Ltd
'Moonrising', Narone Creek Road, Wollombi, NSW 2325, Australia
P.O. Box 60–490, Titirangi, Auckland 0642, New Zealand
www.exislepublishing.com

National Library of Australia Cataloguing-in-Publication Data:

  Skellett, Chris.

  When happiness is not enough : balancing pleasure and achievement in your life / Chris Skellett.

  ISBN 9781921497179 (pbk.)

  Includes bibliographical references and index.

  Happiness.
  Self-actualization (Psychology).
  Conduct of life.

  158.1

Designed by Christabella Designs
Typeset in Bembo 11/18
Printed in Shenzhen, China, by Ink Asia

This book uses paper sourced under ISO 14001 guidelines from well-managed forests and other controlled sources.

The author would like to thank Dr Russ Harris for permission to reproduce the quote from *The Happiness Trap: Stop Struggling, Start Living* (Exisle Publishing, 2007) that appears on page 23.

The images used on pages 75 and 91 are courtesy of iStockphoto.

10 9 8 7 6 5 4 3 2

Disclaimer

When
HAPPINESS
IS NOT
ENOUGH

FOR WHOM THIS BOOK IS WRITTEN

This book has been written for anyone who's feeling a little too fat.
Or who drinks a little too much.

Or for anyone who's recently been told to slow down and relax.
Or who feels stressed.

It's for people who know that they're a little bit lazy.
But it's also for those who know that they're a little intense.

Some wish that they'd done more with their lives.
Others wish that they'd taken more time to play.

These are the people for whom this book is written.

It's a book that invites us all to stop for a moment.
And to think about the choices we make …

Contents

Preface
WHEN HAPPINESS IS NOT ENOUGH

Happiness is such a simple, unifying concept. For most of us, happiness is the general ambition that we hold for ourselves in life. We all want to be happy. We all want to die happy.

But do we really know what happiness is? Do we really understand its complexity? Does the concept of happiness mean the same thing to all of us? Does 'pure joy' lie on the same continuum as 'quiet satisfaction'? And does happiness in itself lead us to live a fulfilling life? In short, as we make our way through life, the simple concept of 'happiness' may not really be defined enough to guide us through the complexities that we face.

This book will help us to discriminate clearly between two fundamental types of happiness. It will help us to know ourselves better, and to make active choices towards a more fulfilling life.

The central theme here is that complete happiness is to be found by blending feelings of sensory *pleasure* with feelings of *satisfaction* through achievement. We should aim to balance the excitable pleasure of the moment with the deeper satisfaction of achieving our established goals in life.

If we can establish a healthy balance between pleasure and achievement for ourselves, then we are more likely to live a fulfilling life. And by applying the 'Pleasure/Achievement Principle' to the lifestyle decisions we make, we will experience a far deeper sense of personal fulfilment in our lives.

Chapter One

AN INTRODUCTION TO THE PLEASURE/ACHIEVEMENT PRINCIPLE

Everybody wants to be happy. We all know when we're happy and when we're sad, and our life is full of decisions made in our search for happiness. We make these decisions from moment to moment and from year to year. And usually, we tend to base our decisions on a generalised theme or preference. For example, we might prefer excitement to comfort, or change rather than stability. These trends and preferences are many and varied, and they can all play out in different ways.

But of all the different factors that drive our decisions and shape our behaviour, there is one simple truth that underpins our complex lives more than any other. Specifically, we need to ensure that in all aspects of our lives, we maintain a healthy balance between *the drive for pleasure* and *the drive for satisfaction through achievement*. Happiness is to be found by combining them both.

The concepts sound so similar, and both feel good, but a closer analysis shows that they are two very different emotions. We tend to use the words 'pleasure' and 'satisfaction' interchangeably, and we do not take due care in distinguishing between the two. 'It gives me great pleasure …' and 'I take great satisfaction …' are two phrases that sound very much the same. But by failing to discriminate, we fail to balance the two concepts and, as a result, we fail in our efforts to live a balanced and fulfilling life.

The secret to living an enjoyable, rewarding life is to balance pleasure and achievement, and to be mindful of the relative importance of these two key drivers.

> The Pleasure/Achievement Principle can be defined thus:
> *In order to live a fulfilling life, we must strike a considered balance between pleasure and achievement.*

Essentially, we need to become more aware of whether we tend to seek pleasure in our lives, or whether we instead strive to experience satisfaction through achieving personal goals. In order to develop our awareness of this issue, we will need to look at the two key concepts in a little more detail.

Pleasure

Pleasure is based on short-term gratification. It's fun, it's indulgent, and it's the basis of humour, enjoyment and a sense of contentment. With pleasure, we live in the moment. We feel alive and we love the sensual delights that are on offer. We relax, we feel comfortable, and we soak up life to the full. Our base instincts are to seek pleasure, and for many, experiencing pleasure is the ultimate goal of a life well lived! We value and define our happiness in this way. *We remember the fun that we've had.*

When we are pleasure focused, life is to be savoured; it is to be appreciated for the way that it is. We are happy to simply enjoy. We feel relaxed, and we look back on a day of pleasurable experiences. *Our smiles are happy smiles.*

Satisfaction

Satisfaction is different. It is based on the achievement of personal goals. We set goals, we achieve them, and we feel satisfied as a result. Satisfaction is usually achieved by overriding the short-term pain and discomfort of action in pursuit of a chosen goal. We dig deep and admire our strength and our energy. We value motivation, drive and ambition. We climb mountains; we win gold. *We remember the things that we've achieved.*

When we are achievement focused, there are always improvements to be made, things to learn and opportunities to explore. We make lists, we work hard, and by the end of the day we are tired. We look back at what we have achieved. *Our smiles are satisfied smiles.*

•

While pleasure tends to be a transient experience, feelings of satisfaction are usually longer lasting. Some of us look for what there is to be enjoyed in the present, right now. Others look ahead to what could be achieved in the future, and they also look back to remember what has been achieved in the past. They value outcomes that occur over time.

Pleasure, achievement and lifestyle problems

When a pleasure focus becomes excessive, we can find ourselves drifting into a variety of unhealthy lifestyles. Pleasurable indulgence can lead to laziness, depressive lethargy, or self-control issues. We show an excess of what psychologists call *consummatory behaviours,* where we 'consume' opportunities for pleasure. We seek comfort and contentment in our lives. We often become complacent with ourselves, and our physical health suffers.

When an achievement focus becomes excessive, however, different problems emerge. The drive to achieve can result in stress, anxiety and a generalised inability to relax or feel good about ourselves. We live *appetitively*, where we are 'hungry' and constantly needing to satisfy our 'appetite' for more. We often carry a generalised restlessness in our daily lives. We are always looking ahead and trying to improve. There is a continual urge to effect change. Life is always full of possibilities, but it can become a tiring theme both for ourselves and for those around us.

Clearly, a number of clinical problems can arise if there is a significant imbalance between pleasure and achievement in our lives.

An excessive focus on pleasure will lead to a certain class of lifestyle problems. Most self-control issues for individuals — such as over-eating, alcohol or substance abuse and gambling — are based on an excessive focus on short-term pleasure. We become over-indulgent.

To counter this, self-control programs will set clear goals for individuals to achieve. We are encouraged to lose weight, to save money or to give up smoking. We keep records and we monitor progress. And when we achieve our goals, we feel satisfied. By exercising self-control, we are essentially re-focusing on experiencing a sense of 'satisfaction' in the longer term, instead of choosing more 'pleasurable' experiences in the shorter term.

Similarly, most programs that promote physical fitness and health will encourage us to make consistent lifestyle decisions based on achievement. These are always referenced towards the achievement of future, satisfying goals, rather than the enjoyment or pleasure of the present moment. In other words, we have to suspend current pleasure in order to achieve greater satisfaction in the future.

We often hear people saying, 'I don't like going to the gym.' But few people ever go to the gym because they enjoy it, or because they find it 'pleasurable'. Instead, they go to 'achieve' fitness and muscle tone. It's hard work. But like work, the key driver for them is the satisfaction experienced at the end of the session. If we happen to enjoy it too, that's great, but it's not the key driver. For most of us, going to the gym is an ultimately satisfying activity if the goals are achieved. But it is rarely a pleasurable activity while you're actually there!

An excessive focus on achievement will create a different class of psychological problems for an individual. There will be an over-emphasis on achieving certain goals or standards. Stress, burnout and obsessive problems all derive from an overvalued desire to achieve. People display an unrelenting drive to improve or to make changes. They seem restless and strive for a satisfaction that is rarely attained. They are so pressured and busy that their relationships suffer. For these people, achievement must be balanced with a greater degree of pleasure in their lives. Essentially, these folk need to learn to stop and 'smell the roses'.

Emotions and the Pleasure/Achievement Principle

Our mood is also determined by the complex interplay between pleasure and achievement. When we feel bored or depressed, we will often eat chocolate, lie in bed and generally indulge ourselves. We feel sad. We want to feel happy. We attempt to compensate for our sadness by treating ourselves to some pleasure. We focus on this form of happiness and try to cheer ourselves up with a good time. But these pleasure-oriented actions serve to give only short-term respite from sadness before we sink back and feel even worse than before.

In contrast to treating ourselves with pleasurable experiences when we feel depressed, we need instead to seek a deeper sense of happiness through satisfaction. The more lasting pathway out of depression is to set simple goals, to establish a sense of purpose, and to aim for a more enduring sense of satisfaction. By taking small, tangible steps towards a more active lifestyle, we achieve a steady accumulation of satisfying experiences. As a result, the passive sense of helplessness that typically characterises a depressive mindset slowly dissipates. In this way, it turns out that seeking satisfaction is the primary antidote to depression, not indulging in gratuitous pleasure.

Paradoxically, an excessive indulgence in pleasure will eventually leave us feeling empty and flat. Life's 'endless party' ceases to be fun and life can seem superficial. There is no momentum, no drive and no sense of fulfilment. We become dissatisfied. We lack motivation or ambition, and ultimately, life can feel pointless.

In Chapter Ten, we will briefly review a range of clinical issues that can arise in everyday life, and that can be usefully considered from a pleasure/achievement perspective.

Ageing with style and purpose

The relevance of pleasure and satisfaction often varies at different stages of our lives. Different generations face different challenges, and common problems and tensions will arise.

Teenagers and students, for example, face the constant dilemma of balancing academic achievement with the more seductive pleasures of partying around town. Their lives can often become based on the unrelenting pursuit of social pleasures, at the expense of study and hard work. But then, at the end of the year, life suddenly becomes all about grades again, and priorities need to be hastily reviewed!

Invariably, decisions at this age are finely balanced between the urge to experience pleasure and the need to achieve. But we do not always recognise our own decision-making patterns in this respect. We do not necessarily see that we have choices. As a result, we simply stumble on through life without much pause for thought.

In addition, teenagers' attitudes are also strongly shaped by the opinions and values of those who surround them. The influence and attitudes of their peers and role models are often a huge factor in shaping their lifestyle values. Their heroes are either highly successful achievers in their chosen field, or else they are highly engaging, charismatic personalities who fascinate us because of *who* they are rather than anything they achieve.

At school, did we prioritise homework or TV? Did we spend our free time in the library, or did we goof off to the park?

As students, did we prefer to spend our time in the library or in the pub? Were we more often found sitting at a desk or lying on the couch? Did we tend to go out on the town or did we choose to have an early night instead?

Usually, unless we are particularly careful, it is those invitations to pleasure that drive our decisions during our young adult years!

During *adult life*, we all find ourselves caught up in an achievement-oriented world. Developing careers, raising children and paying off mortgages all become major themes to our lives. Promotions, social status and the acquisition of wealth become more relevant. Often we resent the pressure, but it's all around us. Every day we are either getting a little further ahead or a little further behind.

But later … at the other end of our adult lives, the pleasure/achievement issue swings around again to the other extreme. In *retirement,* the dilemma suddenly becomes one of learning to disengage from a productive life and instead value the opportunity to sit back and enjoy life for what it has to offer. The transition from pleasure to productivity is again reversed, and we learn to value the simple art of enjoyment once more.

Grumpy old men are usually the direct result of a failure to manage this issue. As they age, they can no longer achieve to the same standard. They become frustrated at their inability to perform to the same levels. For them, there is so much to be gained by simply shifting sideways towards a greater pleasure orientation in their lives, and to just enjoy life for what it is.

In summary, we all tend to struggle with finding the right balance for ourselves during life's transitions. In Chapter Four, we shall be reviewing the role of pleasure and achievement during the seven stages of our lives, and we will reflect on our personal journey so far in order to gain useful insights.

We shall also consider the influence that family, social and cultural values may have in shaping our worldview, and we shall reflect on how these factors may be applied to our own lives.

Finding happiness in each aspect of our lives

Our life falls naturally into three areas: time spent at play, at work and at home. Each area has its own tendency to encourage either achievement or pleasure, and we tend to fall into habitual patterns of behaviour in each domain without a great deal of thought. It becomes second nature for us to strive to win or to just sit back and cruise, whether we are in work mode, play mode or simply at home with family. Sometimes the balance gets lost and, as a result, our experience of life's richness is diminished.

Happiness at play

Our natural tendency towards either pleasure or achievement will play out most obviously in our leisure activities. In reviewing how we prefer to spend our free time, certain themes will quickly become apparent.

For example, on a Saturday morning, we can easily choose to spend our time mowing the lawns, cleaning the car and ticking off jobs from the 'to do' list. This may be our preference. But alternatively, we could choose to spend Saturday mornings kicking back and just cruising around the house. It's the weekend. We want to relax, play music and drink coffee.

The same applies when we plan for a holiday. Do we aim to relax and take an ocean cruise, or do we enrol for an Italian cookery class in Tuscany? Do we camp by a lake and read trashy magazines, or do we take a five-day hike in the mountains? And on our return, do we remember the fun that we've had or the things that we've achieved? Are we more relaxed or are we more knowledgeable as a result of our trip away?

There are no right or wrong decisions here. But we do need to be aware of our preferences, and we need to ensure that we eventually strike a good overall balance.

When we play sport, we can play competitively and become driven to play to our full potential, or we can simply enjoy getting out in the fresh air and having fun. We can go fishing to catch lots of fish, or simply to 'go fishing'. We can play tennis to win, or simply to enjoy ourselves with friends.

Our decisions should normally fall between the two options. If we aren't enjoying activities, then we should seriously review their place in our lives. Similarly, if we're not learning or achieving anything, then we need to review how we are spending our time.

In looking back over a weekend at home or a holiday away, we should always be able to reflect contentedly on both the things that we've achieved *and* on the fun that we've had.

We shall look at the application of the Pleasure/Achievement Principle on our leisure time in more detail in Chapter Seven.

Happiness at work

Activity at work is almost always achievement oriented. We go to work to achieve things. We are paid to produce outcomes at the end of the day. We have a clear sense of purpose.

As an example, we can look at the stereotypical corporate types who strive naturally towards business success. For them, the key drivers are to achieve their monthly targets, their personal KPIs (key performance indicators), and to contribute towards the stated objectives of their organisation. They focus on outputs, achievements and tangible outcomes.

They will often carry over this energetic perspective into their social and recreational lives as well. They are drawn towards events that provide social networking opportunities, climbing ever upwards towards a higher social standing and a higher net worth. They also love to be competitive in their chosen sports. They like to win and they like to be the best!

But all work and no play makes Jack a dull boy! An excessive competitive drive towards achievement at the expense of pleasure can often lead to burnout, stress and anxiety, underpinned by the fear of failure. There is little contentment, little happiness and little joy. There is often a generalised sense of restlessness and dissatisfaction with life. Success is achieved but rarely celebrated. There is always another goal to aim for and another level to reach.

To balance this achievement orientation, it is imperative that we learn to pause, reflect and be more 'in the moment'. We need to be able to be more accepting of how things are, and to appreciate the world for how it is, rather than always looking for improvement and change. We don't need to be always setting goals and making lists. We sometimes just need time to 'be', and to be connected with those around us.

In Chapter Eight, we will review the importance of maintaining a balanced perspective at work, and we will explore ways to make our work life as enjoyable as we can.

Happiness at home

Our behaviour *in family relationships* is also driven by our preference to either:

  a) *achieve* in our lives together, or

  b) simply *enjoy* our lives together.

Usually, our preferences are reasonably aligned with those of our partner. But if we see the world differently, then tensions can quickly evolve. However, if we choose to, we can see these differences as 'complementary', where one person's achievement orientation is balanced by the other's natural ability to relax.

It is important to clarify whether, as partners, we are hoping for our relationship to primarily bring contentment and happiness or for it to bring wealth and success. For example, how shall we plan financially for our lives? Shall we invest and save purposefully for our retirement, or should we live more expansively and enjoy the moment? Ideally, of course, most couples would look to strike a prudent balance between the two.

Paul: 'Since Louise left me, I've just realised that an achievement orientation is all about *doing* things together, while pleasure is all about simply *being* together. Louise and I spent all our time keeping busy and planning ahead. We really needed to take more time just to be together in the moment, and to enjoy what we had. We were totally out of balance in the way that we lived our lives …'

It is also important to consider the degree to which we are looking for 'satisfaction' or for 'pleasure' from each other at an emotional level. A relationship based on achieving mutually satisfying goals (such as social status, job promotion and material wealth) looks and feels very different to a relationship that is based simply on pleasure. It can often appear like harder work to an outsider, with both partners seeming restless, always looking to achieve something more from their life together.

And what about the time spent together in the bedroom? We need to be clear about whether we are just looking to relax and 'enjoy' the pleasure of being together, or whether we are trying to 'achieve' a sense of greater closeness. The subtle difference in language can set up very different expectations.

This is not a discussion topic that couples usually dare to explore, but it could well identify several points of difference that need to be resolved! What exactly is the function of time spent intimately in the bedroom? Is it rather pointless and just a silly giggle or does it serve a more useful function in a couple's life? (You can read more about all this in Chapter Nine.)

•

In summary, the ability to balance our lifestyle decisions is a key life skill. It is the essence of living a happy, satisfying and fulfilling life. It is a defining characteristic of our relationships with partners, friends and colleagues, and it will also affect the way we operate at work, at home and at play.

It is important to ensure that a drive towards objective achievement is always balanced with a more subjective appreciation of the moment, and vice versa. It is also clear that we should stay mindful of our personal tendencies to lean towards either pleasure or satisfaction, and to recognise how this balance might play out in the different areas of our lives.

Whether we are seriously compromised by significant clinical problems or whether we feel that we are just slightly out of balance in our lives, the challenge remains the same for all of us.

By learning to balance decisions that are based on an achievement orientation with decisions that are based on a pleasure orientation, we can choose to live far happier and more rewarding lives.

In later chapters, we shall be reviewing the application of this simple Principle in all aspects of our lives. You will have opportunities to reference the ideas to your own situation, and respond to searching questions that will prompt ideas for change. In Chapter Eleven, you will also have the opportunity to develop your own personal plan.

Balancing pleasure and achievement is obviously a key consideration when planning to live a healthier, more fulfilling life. The Pleasure/ Achievement Principle is a simple yet compelling idea. It is a 'simple truth'. And like many simple truths, it can bring us clarity and an increased sense of personal awareness as we try to manage and make better sense of our busy, complex lives.

Important!

Before you read further, please turn to Appendix 1 and fill out the Pleasure/Achievement Questionnaire. This will give you a broad sense of where you stand on the scale, and will help you to make better use of the rest of this book. As we review the lifestyle issues that arise from applying the Principle, it is useful to know where your own tendency lies.

Chapter Two

A CONTEXT FOR THE PLEASURE/ACHIEVEMENT PRINCIPLE

Before we explore the Pleasure/Achievement Principle in more detail, we need to spend a little time considering a theoretical context for the concept. This chapter is split into two distinct sections that will help us to do just that.

Firstly, we will consider *Values Theory*, in order to become more attuned to the way in which our values broadly shape our lives. Secondly, we will review how *Clinical Psychology Theory* has tended in recent years to shift its focus away from 'goal setting' towards a greater focus on 'acceptance' as a primary theme. Although therapeutic change remains the goal, the emphasis has shifted markedly from striving to achieve behaviour change towards being less judgemental and more appreciative of life's challenges simply for being what they are: challenges. We shift from a focus on *doing* things differently to simply *being* different, and effecting positive personal changes as a result.

The values that shape our lives

Values are curious concepts. They are vaguely defined, essentially subjective and very hard to describe. Yet our underlying values provide the core principles that define the way we live our lives. Whether we are aware of them or not, we make our decisions according to our own, personal, set of values.

Values tend to be derived originally from family rules, cultural norms and social networks. They are refined and honed further by our unique personal experiences, which tend to shape our individual beliefs and perspectives. In short, our values help us to make sense of the world.

There is no finite list of values. Neither is there a list of right values and wrong values. For every value that sounds positive, there is usually an equally valid opposite. This especially applies to values that relate to our lifestyle. We may value firmness but others value flexibility. Some value the expression of forthright opinions, while others value discretion. A preference for independence can be countered by a preference for sociability, tradition by innovation … and so on.

> Knowing the values that guide our behaviour is an important part of self-awareness. This knowledge then allows us to become more mindful of the inherent strengths and weaknesses of our personal styles.

Typically, there are certain values to which we all tend to subscribe. These include honesty, respect, fairness, trust and openness. Often these are referred to as 'Christian' values, whether we formally belong to a Christian church or not. And of course, these values invariably apply universally across the full range of religious faiths. Essentially, they are broad concepts of interpersonal behaviour that are used to define ethical conduct in a civilised society.

Values are often specified quite clearly in political affiliations, community groups or codes of conduct for organisations. There will be a charter or a defining document that explicitly states what the values of the organisation are. It becomes a commitment to behave in a certain way, and in a sense, becomes the glue or cohesive theme that binds members together. We are drawn to groups that hold values that are congruent with our own.

Within these formal frameworks, however, there is a multitude of individual or group differences that provides a richness and variety to society. But these differences can also cause confusion and irritation between people. Those who value orderliness and structure can often come into conflict with those who value flexible and more casual arrangements. Similarly, those who value innovation may clash with those who value conservatism. Pragmatists will often clash with idealists, and those who champion the 'passionate heart' will find themselves challenged by the actions of those whose key driver is the 'logical mind'.

Know thy values, know thyself!

We attempt to resolve most conflicts or disagreements in life by arguing about the other person's logic. However, the logic is rarely flawed. Usually, the difference of opinion is simply based on a difference in underlying values. It's the way that we see the world, and the way that we believe it should be, that drives conflict. The logical argument is then based upon this. Politicians, economists and academics critique each other's logic all the time, but it is invariably a difference in core values and beliefs that actually underpins the problem.

In the context of the current discussion, there is often a tension between those who want to work hard and make a difference, and those who want to enjoy life and have fun. This debate can polarise quickly. And while we can all relate at different times to either side of a values debate, it helps us enormously to know what our key drivers are, and how to use them to maximum effect.

Among all of the 'values dichotomies' that have been mentioned so far, there is none that drives our lifestyle quite so fundamentally as that implicit in the Pleasure/Achievement Principle. In essence, *as individuals do we value the drive to achieve or do we value the experience of pleasure?*

Question 1

When considering your life overall, do you tend to value the drive to achieve or do you tend to value the experience of pleasure?

Question 2

What does the concept of personal growth mean to you? Do you strive to 'know yourself better' or do you strive to be 'a better person'?

In different situations and at different times, we are obliged to make decisions based on this balance between pleasure and achievement. We must be careful not to play excessively to our preferred style, and instead must learn to make conscious decisions to find a 'best fit' for ourselves under the circumstances.

It is often the case that our greatest strengths can become our greatest weaknesses. Regardless of which side of the balance we lean towards, our preference can easily develop and strengthen in a way that takes us out to unhealthy extremes. Those who appreciate pleasure tend to become increasingly and perhaps excessively indulgent, whilst those who value achievement can become excessively 'driven' and pressured in their lives.

The key reason for clarifying our personal values is to increase our awareness and to ensure that we live life in balance.

How psychologists see the Pleasure/Achievement Principle

The Pleasure/Achievement Principle is a concept that fits very neatly into recent trends in clinical psychology. Although the primary focus for psychologists is on resolving a variety of problems of everyday living, finding 'happiness' is usually seen as the generic antidote.

The study of happiness has waxed and waned over the years, with biochemistry often seen as a major factor. However, happiness is clearly based on positive self-talk or perhaps can be seen as a 'mental habit'. Thinking positively is a state of mind that should probably be the paramount goal of all therapeutic work.

To achieve this, clinical psychologists have historically based their treatments and counselling styles on a very pragmatic, goal-oriented approach. Initially, they focused on changing behavioural patterns, with the assumption that if you behaved differently then your thoughts and your feelings would change too.

The *behavioural* approach in the 1960s proved to be revolutionary in providing effective treatments to a wide variety of problems. Psychological problems were formulated in terms of dysfunctional behavioural patterns, and subsequent goals for behaviour change were set. Underlying reasons for the problems were given little attention. The basic idea was that if you simply changed behaviour, then the subjective feelings would change too. Depression was formulated as an absence of positive, active behaviours. The theory was that if we made ourselves do pleasurable things, then we would become happier. If we laughed more, then we would feel better. If we set goals to socialise, then we would become more sociable.

'Menus' of pleasurable activities were drawn up to use as goal-setting sheets, such as the Pleasant Events Schedule (MacPhillamy and Lewinsohn, 1973), or the Reinforcement Survey Schedule (Cautela and Kastenbaum, 1967). These lists included rather obvious activities such as eating ice cream, listening to Country and Western music, looking at interesting buildings, looking at beautiful people, playing tennis, and doing crosswords. Interestingly, the items on these menus could have been divided easily into either pleasurable experiences or satisfying activities, but instead were all thrown together indiscriminately.

A behavioural menu/checklist can seem a rather amusing approach to finding happiness now, but the original intention was good and the treatment seemed effective. People chose activities from the list and promised to experience them as homework before the next session. They became happier because of the experiences they were scheduling for themselves.

In the late 1970s and early '80s, this behavioural approach was extended to include the realm of thought, where unhelpful thinking patterns were seen as similarly dysfunctional to the behavioural habits that define problems. Clients were still encouraged to set goals, but this time they were asked to focus on changing their thoughts as well as their behaviour. This approach was called *Cognitive Behavioural Therapy* (CBT) and later evolved into *Cognitive Therapy* (Aaron Beck, 1976). To feel happy, one needed to do fun activities and think happy thoughts. The theory was that our thoughts and behaviours drive our emotional state.

CBT remained the treatment of choice for many psychological problems such as anxiety and depression. Over the next decade, CBT became more sophisticated. It developed from a simple analysis of the superficial thoughts that we are aware of into a deeper consideration of the underlying assumptions or beliefs that organise and drive these thoughts. Underlying assumptions, of course, are impossible to measure or record and are hugely subjective. The commitment to scientific objectivity that was the strength of the behavioural approach was slowly evolving into a more speculative affair.

This level of analysis became increasingly popular in the 1990s as techniques to challenge enduring patterns of dysfunctional thinking were developed. These ideas were best captured by Dr Jeffrey Young's *Schema Therapy* (Young, 1994).

In Schema Therapy, all the goal-setting structures were retained from the original behavioural approach, but were now applied to a very abstract, covert level of psychological process. To capture this approach in a single phrase, Jeff Young talked about clients who carried dysfunctional 'prejudiced beliefs' that biased their view of themselves and the world around them. If you could challenge the dysfunctional belief (for example, that people can't be trusted) then you could resolve the problem. In his book *Reinventing Your Life*, Young describes sixteen specific schema, or dysfunctional beliefs, that can generate pervasive problems in people's lives.

The most recent step in the evolution of psychological approaches began towards the end of the 1990s, when a new 'wave' of psychological therapies based on 'mindfulness' began to emerge. These approaches now provide the cutting edge for new clinical techniques. Foremost among these new theoretical approaches is *Acceptance and Commitment Therapy* or ACT (Steven Hayes, 2005).

The key conceptual change in the ACT approach is that *instead of challenging and fighting a problem, we instead simply accept its presence* and move forward regardless in a valued direction. Actual behavioural or lifestyle change is still the end result, but the process is very different. There is a very close parallel to Buddhist teachings of acceptance here, which would have seemed unthinkable to clinicians only 30 years ago!

Arriving at an approach that is similar to traditional Buddhist teachings formed over many thousands of years may seem like a convoluted and unnecessary journey. But then there are very few original simple truths to be discovered in this world.

Every new approach has merit in its own time. In a sense, we are simply coming to the same truth in a different way at a different time. Wise folk will often say that you never swim in the same river twice ... and they'd be right!

The Primary Focus of Therapy Approaches Over the Years		
Therapy Approach	Pleasure/Experiential Focus?	Achievement/Outcome Focus?
Behavioural	No	Yes
Cognitive Behavioural	No	Yes
Cognitive	No	Yes
Schema Therapy	Yes	Yes
Acceptance and Commitment Therapy	Yes	No

ACT has become a very popular model, and in his bestselling book, *The Happiness Trap*, Dr Russ Harris describes the approach and challenges the old assumption that we can 'find' happiness by searching it out. Instead, he points out that happiness is all around us. Embedded within his book is a great definition of happiness. He describes happiness not just as 'a sense of pleasure, gladness or gratification', but also as being underpinned by experiencing 'a rich, full and meaningful life' in which we 'feel the full range of human emotions, both the painful ones and the pleasant ones'. This latter sense of 'meaning' is an experience derived from acting in a valued or worthy way. We are 'living purposefully towards valued objectives'.

Within the pleasure/achievement context, the first type of happiness that is described is similar to the concept of 'pleasure'. The second type of happiness is the same as the concept of 'satisfaction' that we get from achieving our (valued) goals.

Fundamentally, therefore, the language of psychological therapy has gradually changed. Instead of 'challenging' problem thoughts and behaviours and setting goals for change, we are now invited to notice and 'accept' patterns of thinking and behaviour, in effect 'disempowering' them.

By noticing one's troublesome thoughts as a detached observer, we learn to disassociate from them and they lose their impact.

Psychologists remain concerned with the study of 'thought'. For cognitive therapists, and for most of us in our everyday worlds, the chattering noise in our heads represents who we are. As Descartes said many years ago, 'I think, therefore I am.' A close variation is to say, 'I am what I think.' It is hard for us to detach from our thoughts and to simply notice the bias in the commentary that is going on in our heads about the world around us. However, a wonderfully cautionary line from the ACT literature also suggests that 'your mind is not always your friend'. Your mind does not always act in your best interests. It can undermine and diminish you as a person. So regardless of whether we directly confront our thoughts or simply become more mindful of them, the challenge remains the same. We need to become more self-aware of our thinking biases, and we need to take greater control over them in our everyday lives.

Therapy conversations between clinical psychologists and their clients these days will usually involve drawing up a treatment plan that focuses on:

a) setting clear goals for behavioural or cognitive change (and looking for motivation to get there), or

b) encouraging a greater acceptance of the way things are, not judging or evaluating, and learning to be comfortable in your own skin.

As potential clients, we will all tend to choose a therapy framework that provides a 'best fit' to our preferred orientation, and work in the style that feels comfortable and familiar to us. However, in choosing a therapy approach, we sometimes might like to consider developing our less preferred orientation. In this case, we would then decide to deliberately work in our less preferred mode. Goal setting will be a challenging experience for those with a pleasure orientation, while mindfulness will be a challenging experience for those with an achievement orientation.

Regardless of the theoretical orientation of our therapist, it is important that during our therapy conversations we become more aware of how personal thinking biases may be holding us back. Different psychological theories appeal to different people at different times, but there is always much to be gained by staying open to the benefits of alternative perspectives. Both goal setting and acceptance are equally popular theoretical starting points for therapy, and both have their strengths. Neither approach is right or wrong; they are simply different. More importantly, they appeal to different sides of the pleasure/achievement continuum.

Key points to take from this chapter

- In this chapter, we have looked at the role that our inherent *values* system plays in our life. We saw that general themes will play out in our lives in accordance with our established values. More specifically, we saw how the degree to which we value either pleasure or achievement can become a dominant theme in our lifestyle.
- We considered how the Pleasure/Achievement Principle fits within recent developments in wider *psychological theories*. In general terms, we saw how the Principle sits comfortably across the two current therapy approaches of choice: 'behavioural goal setting' and 'mindfulness'.

Chapter Three
ACTING IN BALANCE, THINKING IN BALANCE, LIVING IN BALANCE

In this chapter, we shall consider how the Pleasure/Achievement Principle plays out at three different levels of our lives. Firstly, we will review how our preference drives the way we *behave* on a daily basis. Then we will look at how it colours the way that we *think* and view the world. Finally, we will look at how our tendency towards pleasure or achievement defines our broad *lifestyle patterns,* and shapes the way we live our lives.

Acting in balance

Have you ever stood in a queue and waited for the person in front of you to stop chatting to the bank clerk, the barmaid or the checkout operator? Has it occurred to you that they should not be making idle chitchat, but instead be getting on with the job of serving their customers?

This is a great example of where a personal preference for a pleasurable interaction overrides the basic need for the person to efficiently complete the task in hand.

Conversely, have you ever been served in a restaurant by a stony-faced waitress who just wants to take your order and move on? Have you been left wanting her to spend just a little more time setting the scene, telling you a bit more about the restaurant, the menu and perhaps a little about her own interests? And wouldn't you have liked to share a little more about why you are there and who you all are?

In the former case, we have a person who is valuing a pleasurable exchange over achieving efficiency. In the latter case, we have the reverse: a goal-oriented achiever who is focused and efficient but who doesn't really value the need for customer rapport. The relationship lacks warmth and the pleasure of the experience is the lesser for it.

Either way, there is an opportunity to bring balance to the situation. Being aware of one's personal preference in these matters allows us to either 'sharpen up' or 'loosen up' in our professional dealings with others.

We like our doctors and dentists to be friendly but efficient. Brief self-disclosures and exchanges of opinion are fine, but essentially, we are there for them to get on with the job. We are there for a purpose and we want successful outcomes.

Conversely, with hairdressers or beauticians, there is a greater expectation to chat and relax as we go. We like them to schedule things so that we can relax a little with them, have a coffee and feel good. Of course we want to see the great haircut at the end, but we generally put an equal emphasis on how enjoyable we found the process. It's not so much that she or he is a great hairdresser, but that she or he is 'really nice'.

So what is the *key difference* between the two styles?

If we think about the examples given above, then we see that it is largely a matter of timeliness. The drive to achieve goals invariably sets a timeline for us and defines an end point. In contrast, the desire to experience pleasure usually asks us to suspend reference to time and to simply lose ourselves in the moment. We try just 'to be'. If it's pleasurable, we wish that it could go on forever and ever. We love to soak in the bath or lie on the beach. But if we're striving for a goal or outcome, then we want to get there as quickly as we can. We build the wall, we dig the ditch, and we run the race.

For pleasure seekers, there is a tendency to make islands of time for relaxation. But for achievers, the tendency is to create a greater awareness of time as a finite resource, and for time to be managed carefully. The phrase 'achieving closure' on an activity or a conversation becomes very important to achievement-oriented individuals. For achievers, everything, absolutely everything, has a beginning, a middle and an end.

Question 1

Do you need to tighten up or loosen up with regard to timeliness? Think of a practical example.

Question 2

What changes could you make in your life to:
a) enjoy more quality time?
b) make better use of your time?

It would be unusual to find someone who was totally committed to one side or other of the pleasure/achievement scale. The concepts of pleasure and achievement essentially describe two classes of activity. There are those activities characterised by pleasure, and those characterised by satisfaction. We all experience both to varying degrees, despite tending to show a preference for one or the other.

We will often compensate for an excessive focus on achievement at work by becoming over-indulgent at home. But if work is dull and lacking in purpose, we may compensate by taking up a more achievement-oriented hobby or interest, such as becoming a sports coach.

It becomes very interesting when we start to review the occurrence of these two classes of activity in our lives, regardless of how much time we spend on one side or other of the line. The overall question to ask ourselves is: 'Where do our priorities lie?' And then we need to ask: 'Have we got the balance right?'

Scheduling activities

As a general rule, it is considered to be healthier to schedule pleasurable activities *after* having achieved a goal (i.e. as a reward). We work hard all week and then we relax and enjoy the weekends. We feel like we've deserved it.

Similarly, suggesting that children tidy up their room before dinner is a natural parenting plan. It is far more effective than the converse, where tidying up *after* dinner is a huge struggle all round. This is the fundamental rule of the behavioural approach to parenting, where we always schedule pleasurable rewards to follow the achievement of a desired outcome.

If you don't eat your meat, then you can't have your pudding ...

This was, of course, an old-fashioned parenting rule popularised by the rock group Pink Floyd in their classic album *The Wall*. It is a simple truth. As kids, we all struggled to eat our meat and vegetables before we were then allowed to eat our dessert. We learned to eat the healthy, nutritious food, and only then could we indulge ourselves in a little pleasure. It is a principle to which we all generally subscribe.

When children have homework, the same principle applies. If they watch TV and then do their homework, there is heaviness in the air all evening until the work has been done. But if they do their homework first, and so earn the privilege of watching TV later, then there is a greater sense of satisfaction and purpose to the evening. The structure feels better all round.

Similarly, if you have achieved great things after a day in the garden, then a cold beer or a glass of wine feels good as a reward. But if you start your day with a beer, then the chances are that you will find it hard to get motivated. You will tend to feel slightly behind the eight ball all day, and will be unlikely to end up with a feeling of satisfaction. And the lawns might not get mown!

For those of us with a pleasure focus, there is an added tendency to *procrastinate*. This means that you are putting off the more demanding tasks that would ultimately bring you satisfaction in favour of a more comfortable option. Procrastination can almost be defined as a situation where 'pleasure consistently overrides achievement as the driver of a decision'. Nothing gets done, and eventually, it will feel like you have wasted the day.

For those with an overriding achievement focus, there is always more to be done. The list of tasks is endless and there often seems to be no time to stop and enjoy the fruits of one's labour. Pausing to enjoy a moment can seem like a waste of time. Life can become a treadmill.

Clearly, the obvious and well-known truth about scheduling events and establishing a healthy relationship with both pleasure and achievement in your daily life is important. Eating a large meal and then having to 'walk it off' seems like something of a penance. But going for a walk to 'work up an appetite' is an altogether different experience. You feel keener and more deserving. It feels healthier, even though it's the same two activities that have been undertaken. The scheduling is different, and this is a key consideration as we review how to live our lives in balance.

In summary, it's a good idea to reward personal achievement with subsequent pleasurable experiences. It just doesn't work the other way around. It's as simple as that.

Question 1

Think of an example where you tend to feel sluggish and procrastinate. What simple changes could you make to your daily schedule that would help you get things done?

Question 2

Think of a situation where you never seem to be able to stop for a breath. How could you build in opportunities to pause and celebrate what's been achieved?

Thinking in balance

Of all of the sections in this book, none is as important as this one. Becoming aware of our self-talk, and how it affects our worldview, sits at the heart of cognitive psychology. The language that we use to interpret the world sets the scene for our appraisal of it. We can say to ourselves, 'This is a boring room' or 'This is a relaxing room'. It's the same room, but by using an emotive adjective, we set ourselves up for a different emotional response.

Our thoughts will determine how we feel.

If we see the world as scary, then we become scared. If we say that it's hopeless, then we feel hopeless. Negative self-talk becomes self-fulfilling, and a half-empty glass will always seem half-empty rather than half-full. Recognising and challenging negative self-talk is the cornerstone of most psychological therapy.

If we consider self-talk in respect of pleasure and achievement, we quickly notice two very different types of narrative.

Pleasure-oriented people will say, 'I want to do this' or 'I'd like to do this'. They scan their world for pleasurable options from which they can choose. Their primary style is to decide what suits them best and what will be the most enjoyable way to spend their time. In the absence of positive options for pleasure, however, they will describe boredom. Their sentence construction is always based around *current* positive and negative emotions.

Conversely, *achievement-oriented* people tend to see the world as a sea of tasks, challenges and obligations. They will tend to use the words 'I should', 'I ought' or 'I must'. There is a lesser sense of choice, and things *have* to get done regardless of what they might want to do instead.

Achievement-oriented people tend to make reference to a sense of duty or what is 'right', rather than simply doing what they would like to do. They focus on what *needs* to be done. Their sentence construction is based around *future positive emotions*, and tends to be conditional in nature — 'If I do this, then I'll feel good'.

To consider this in a practical sense, we might imagine a pleasure-oriented person waking up on a Saturday morning, then deciding that they *want* to have a lie-in before getting up and perhaps phoning a friend to see what they're up to. They see a world of pleasurable options where everything else can be put off until tomorrow.

In contrast, an achievement-oriented person might wake up, then get dressed quickly because they *have* to empty the dishwasher, put on a load of washing, check their emails, and mow the lawn before it rains. They see a world of things to do and tasks to achieve. They are the people who leap to their feet after a meal to wash the dishes (because they 'ought to'), while others sit and enjoy the warm feeling in their tummies (because they 'want to').

The single most important change that anyone can make around pleasure and achievement is simply to change the chatter in their heads! Even though they often face the same set of daily activities, they can either choose to adopt a positive goal-oriented approach that energises and motivates, or else choose a softer, more pleasure-oriented approach that views any activity as a 'sensual feast'.

Even washing the dishes can feel good! Enjoy the warm soapy water, the sparkling clean glasses and the sweet lemony smell of the detergent. It can be a pleasurable experience, while it is obviously also a satisfying experience when completed. And if you play it cleverly, you can gain the benefit of both perspectives.

It is very much up to the individual concerned how they view the activities that they undertake. One person's chore is another's joy.

Remember the scene in *The Adventures of Tom Sawyer* where Tom has to paint a fence as a punishment but manages to convince his friends, including Huckleberry Finn, that it's fun and that they could pay him to have a go if they want?

Which style of thinking sounds most like you?

1) 'I really *should* write those Christmas cards today. I *must* work out what presents people need, and I *ought* to buy them before the shops get too crowded. This year, I've really *got* to try and find more bargains and make sure that I get them away before the cut-off date for posting overseas.'
or
2) 'I love Christmas. This year, I'd really *like* to buy some cool presents for people. Next time I'm in town, I *want* to have a look around and see if there's anything I'd like to buy for them. Whatever happens, I know that I'll *enjoy* shopping for everyone. It's great to be thinking about family and friends in this way.'

Cognitive therapists focus pretty much on changing the way that we 'talk to ourselves' about our worlds. They will challenge a dysfunctional bias in our self-talk.

An excessive achievement orientation will be underpinned by a thinking pattern that continually sets high standards and overly ambitious goals. A degree of generalised tension becomes almost inevitable. There is an expectation that there is always something more to do. This style of self-talk needs to become more forgiving. Achievers need to learn to say to themselves: *'I can relax!'* or *'That's good enough.'*

An excessive pleasure orientation is usually underpinned by more passive self-talk. This focuses on the absorption of good times. Pleasure seekers think about listening to good music, eating fine food and having fun with friends. There is a passive theme to their perception of the world. They don't think about learning to play a new instrument, trying new recipes or working purposefully with their friends. They like to enjoy what is happening around them.

There will be little positive self-talk around self-control and, in general, they will take less responsibility for what happens to them. Pleasure seekers need to use more empowering and assertive self-talk. They need to learn to say to themselves: *'I can make things happen!'* or *'I can make a choice.'*

Listening to the style of one's own self-talk is the most useful thing a person can do in terms of personal growth. If we recognise a bias in our thinking patterns, then it might be useful to consider whether this is helpful to us or not. Cognitive flexibility, or the ability to play both sides of the pleasure/achievement continuum, is a key attribute for those seeking to live a more fulfilling life.

Living in balance

We have now looked at how the ways in which we behave and think can influence the way in which we live our lives. In pulling these ideas together, we can now consider how our overall lifestyle can become twisted by imbalance. To do this, we will need to understand the Pleasure/Achievement Lifestyle Matrix.

The Pleasure/Achievement Lifestyle Matrix

We have noted earlier that pleasure and achievement are not polar opposites and do not necessarily lie neatly in two different boxes. It is not a simple either/or dichotomy; individuals can show varying degrees of both a pleasure orientation and an achievement orientation in their lives. Although a strong achievement orientation will probably come at the expense of pleasure, and vice versa, this is not necessarily the case.

The Pleasure/Achievement Lifestyle Matrix allows us to consider how high and low ratings of pleasure and achievement can interact with each other.

In general, we can rate ourselves as either *high* or *low* on pleasure and *high* or *low* on achievement. We can then draw up a simple matrix of *high* and *low* options for each of these two factors, and this will provide us with a simple table of four possible lifestyle options. These are shown below.

The Pleasure/Achievement Lifestyle Matrix

		PLEASURE	
		LOW	HIGH
A C H I E V E M E N T	HIGH	A DRIVEN LIFESTYLE	A FULFILLING LIFESTYLE
	LOW	A STAGNANT LIFESTYLE	AN INDULGENT LIFESTYLE

The matrix allows us to see at a glance what the four main lifestyle options are, depending on the strength of each factor for an individual. We can consider where we might fit personally (perhaps with reference to our questionnaire scores in Appendix 1).

This is only a very general guide of course, and we can easily apply the model to different parts of our lives and come up with different conclusions. It is really only the broad concept that is important for us to understand at this stage.

The four lifestyles that derive from the matrix are described in more detail below.

A stagnant lifestyle — low pleasure, low achievement

As the name implies, a stagnant lifestyle is not to be envied. There is little appreciation of pleasure in an individual's life, and they do not strive to achieve either. They are stuck passively in a rather dull world where there is little to enjoy. The individual's tendency would have been to answer, 'I don't care' on the Pleasure/Achievement Questionnaire. This is a flat lifestyle, where there is little enjoyment and little satisfaction. The only positive thing that can be said is that at least there is plenty of opportunity for personal development!

A driven lifestyle — low pleasure, high achievement

A significant percentage of the population will describe themselves as 'driven'. They are always on the go and don't find that they get much time to relax. It's a common complaint about modern life. We're all too busy. Challenging the driven lifestyle requires us to slow down and allow time for more pleasure. If we deliberately schedule more pleasure into our lives, we will experience a healthier lifestyle balance, which will become more fulfilling.

An indulgent lifestyle — high pleasure, low achievement

Most individuals who are dissatisfied with their lives would probably call themselves indulgent. Sure there are lots of pleasures to enjoy, but something is missing. No matter how much TV, chocolate cake or wine you consume, you will never feel satisfied. Increasingly, you will feel sluggish and lacking in drive or motivation. Achievement needs to become an identifiable new theme in your life, to provide balance and help you feel fulfilled.

A fulfilling lifestyle — high pleasure, high achievement

Theoretically, this is the ideal state. We are making things happen while also enjoying the experience. We are working hard and playing hard. Literally, we are living life to the full. The only question to ask here is whether it is sustainable. Despite living our life in a healthy balance, are we pushing ourselves too hard?

Of the four lifestyle options listed below, which one fits you best?
• Stagnant
• Driven
• Indulgent
• Fulfilling

Now turn to Chapter Eleven and record your answer.

Key points to take from this chapter

• We have considered three applications of the Pleasure/Achievement Principle. We have broadly reviewed *the behavioural attributes* of both orientations, and then looked at *the cognitive attributes*. Very different patterns of behaviour and thinking quickly become apparent as characteristic of the two distinctive styles. These can be seen as either strengths or weaknesses, and need to be managed with care.

• By assigning ourselves to a quadrant in the Pleasure/Achievement Lifestyle Matrix, we can identify a broad lifestyle pattern for ourselves. It then becomes clear what changes we might need to make to add value to our lives, and to feel a greater sense of personal fulfilment. Do we need more pleasure or more achievement in our lives, or perhaps both?

Important!

Remember to turn to Chapter Eleven, and enter your Pleasure/ Achievement Lifestyle Matrix self-assessment description in the space provided.

Chapter Four
THE INFLUENCE OF TIME AND PLACE

In this chapter, we shall consider how the drive to achieve and the focus on pleasure generally plays out over a typical lifespan. We shall also look at how our cultural, social and family environments come to shape our preferences.

Pleasure, achievement and the seven stages of life

There is no simple template to describe how the balance between pleasure and achievement plays out over a lifetime. Everyone is different. However, what follows is a broad-brush account of the general themes that usually characterise each of the seven stages of life.

There are certain common themes that come to the fore at each developmental stage, and it is well worth reflecting on how the balance may shift over time. As you read on, try to notice the similarities and differences with your own life so far, and with the behaviour of the people around you.

Stage 1: The infancy/preschool years

The life of a neonate is driven entirely by the quest for sensual relief. Babies cry. To a baby, the world seems harsh. They require warmth, full tummies and clean nappies. *The drive for 'pleasure' and comfort is paramount.* Pleasure is found almost passively, simply by signalling discomfort and cuing a parent to alleviate it. By avoiding unpleasant or noxious stimulation, newborn babies are focused entirely on comfort and pleasure.

A smiling, contented baby is indeed a wondrous thing! The drive to re-experience such absolute contentment in later life will, of course, become a pleasure seeker's dream. These moments of perfect pleasure are pure bliss.

After several weeks of this, a baby gradually starts to make connections with its surroundings. Eyes slowly begin to make sense of the world and limb coordination gets underway. While not exactly setting goals at this stage, a baby will start to reach out to touch things. It will gradually become more purposeful in its movements and will become increasingly aware of the consequences to activity. This key aspect of neonatal development (when a baby discovers that behaviour has consequences) lays down *the fundamental platform for an achievement-oriented life.* The conditional nature of the world ('If I do this, then that will happen') quickly becomes a guiding principle for achievers.

The developmental milestones in early childhood are hugely significant. The first smile, the first word and the first step are all great achievements. The first step especially can assume an overwhelming significance for both children and parents alike. The value placed on that first, purposeful step towards something, however irrelevant, remains embedded in parents' memories forever. They clap. They applaud. They exuberantly celebrate the child's ability to achieve.

In contrast to these early pacesetters, there is another class of babies who perhaps lie more quietly, smiling peacefully at those around them. They are in no hurry to explore or to challenge, but nevertheless are quietly making sense of their world. They watch, they absorb information, and their parents proudly admire their placid, contented personalities. They 'go down easy', they have good appetites and they sleep through the night. They play happily with the toys they are given, in contrast to their counterparts who seem to always be searching restlessly for the next big thing.

As they grow, all children tend to explore their world with an increasing curiosity. There seems to be an innate drive and motivation to explore, and with each discovery, new horizons appear. Learning accelerates on all fronts, as verbal, intellectual and interpersonal skills develop. An excitable interaction evolves between the drive to succeed and the pleasurable celebration of that success, and parenting style clearly plays a huge part in determining where the emphasis is placed.

For some families, pride in the achievements of their children is the paramount emotion. Parents focus on physical, social and academic milestones. In other families, the parents love to share stories about how their children *are*. They share anecdotes about their emerging personalities, their charm and endearing features. Most of their family photos illustrate smiling, happy children rather than earnest, triumphant children. For them, fun and happiness are more strongly held childhood values.

Stage 2: The school years

At school, the more formal educational structures and the academic emphasis on measurement tip the balance firmly towards an achievement focus. We leave behind the non-judgemental world of potato cuts and finger paintings (where everything is great!) to find ourselves comparing and contrasting with each other.

The concepts of success and failure enter rapidly into the equation and increasingly children are invited to strive for achievement. Even if the current education system tries to minimise the competitive nature of relationships between children in the classroom, they are still encouraged to benchmark themselves against their existing abilities, and to improve.

Children are invited to set goals for themselves that draw them forward. In the sporting, academic and cultural spheres, certificates, trophies and scholarships abound. There is a tendency to feel proud to be the cleverest, the fittest and the most popular. We also learn to covet the successes of others if they win. Jealousies and disappointments can often arise.

In the world of education, everything is measured, and this introduces an inherent evaluative component to our self-image. We learn to ask ourselves whether we are good enough. Could we do better?

Stage 3: Adolescence/the student years

As puberty strikes, the appeal of a pleasure orientation rears up again. Hormones kick in and we dreamily indulge in idle rumination. We are drawn to artistic statements. Music, art and the theatre all capture moments for us, and we feel inspired simply by the way that we feel. The world becomes a sea of here-and-now experiences to be savoured. Teenagers collectively enjoy life. They enjoy drinking together, dancing together, laughing together and being generally goofy together.

During this phase, ambition and drive can come under serious threat as it suddenly becomes 'cool' to hang out aimlessly. Hours and hours can be spent in front of a screen, soaking up TV cartoons, YouTube clips and mindless computer games. In passing, it should be noted that television has opted massively to reinforce the *pleasure-seeking aspect* of our natures. Broadcasts are usually classified as 'entertainment'. There is minimal programming to encourage learning or personal development, and we rarely switch off TV feeling satisfied with the way that we have spent our time. It's an indulgent pleasure … and teenagers love it.

For teenagers, strong emotions of love, anger and hopelessness can quickly arise, and tend to become major drivers of their conduct. The short-term indulgence of emotional release becomes a strong theme to most teenagers' lives, and here, of course, we are also talking about sex. Achieving self-control over pleasurable opportunity is generally not high on the agenda for this age group!

But meanwhile, parents and teachers will continue to champion an achievement ethic. Higher school grades, honours in representative sport and academic prizes all become cherished goals. Living a purposeful, goal-directed life does not come easy at this age, however, and conflicted teenagers can often struggle to establish a healthy balance of pleasure and achievement during these turbulent years.

The dilemmas of the teenage years are later compounded when young people strike out independently and redefine themselves as 'students'. If the transition to tertiary training also involves leaving home, then the students are suddenly freed from their family values. They are now obliged to make their own choices for creating a balance between study and social excess. Will they choose to spend time at the library or will they go to the bar? Will they go to the gym or go for a coffee with friends? Will they do the washing or will they watch TV? Choices, choices … Should they achieve or should they enjoy?

For many students, life revolves around beds, couches and screens, but miraculously, by the end of their training they suddenly seem to come right and graduate calmly, as if it was always meant to be! They surge on into the workforce with an emergent sense of purpose, drive and motivation to achieve.

Stage 4: Building a family and career

After graduation, or on completion of a workforce training program, there is usually a distinct change of gear. As the twenty-somethings enter the workforce, usually on the bottom rung of a career ladder, they suddenly become more purposeful in their relationships.

As young people commit to their partners, there is an inherent vision of how their future together might broadly look. They might dream of owning a house in the country, of having kids, or perhaps travelling overseas. These broad plans then necessarily require them to set more specific, practical objectives.

They will start to save money rather than spend it. They set timelines for achieving certain goals, and they start to acquire both tangible assets and intangible responsibilities and skill sets. They compare their progress with that of their peer group, and there is a generalised competitiveness with regard to 'getting on' in life. Young couples building a life together are more likely to be preoccupied with their 'success' rather than their 'happiness'.

My hairdresser, Sonya, was pregnant with her second child. I asked her if she was looking forward to giving birth again.

'Well, I couldn't really say that childbirth is fun,' she replied. 'But it certainly has to be one of the most satisfying experiences that a woman can ever have.'

Even as a man, I knew exactly what she meant.

While opportunities abound in this phase of life, it can be an extremely stressful time. The achievement focus can easily get out of hand as we strive towards a better life. Security is a concept to work towards rather than something that is felt. People spend a great deal of their twenties trying to get to a certain point by the time they are 30. The years flash by.

Stage 5: The mid-life plateau

There comes a time in mid-life when we start to plateau. We slowly resign ourselves to our lot. If we are single, then we expect to continue that way. If we are in a relationship and we are happy enough with our partner and kids, then we will probably settle for continuing with the way things are. At work, we find that we have risen to a level of responsibility where we don't expect to go much higher, and we accept that this is probably 'as good as it gets'.

Of course, some people don't accept this so easily, and then we witness all the restless upheavals of separation, dramatic changes of career, and all the personal disappointments that result from a sense of failing to fulfil the expectations that were set earlier in life.

Ideally, mid-life should be a great phase for us, whatever our situation. It is a time when we can take off the pressure, enjoy the children (or lack of them), and maintain a healthy work–life balance. We at last have the time to appreciate the richness of what life has to offer. We have established a secure platform upon which we can be who we want to be. We no longer need to prove ourselves at work or drive ourselves along at pace. Instead, we can develop a greater awareness of those around us and draw out the best in them.

This is often a time when opportunities for leadership occur, both at work, in the family and in the community. The emphasis is not so much on what we can achieve for ourselves, but instead on what we can inspire in those around us. Some of us embrace leadership opportunities with both hands and achieve great things. For others, we simply want to relax and enjoy the benefits gained from the efforts that we have made to get to this point.

'To cruise or not to cruise', that is the question! In mid-life, there is plenty of room for our preferences to play out in myriad ways. We have more choice and we have more options.

Stage 6: Later adult life

After several years of knowing that we have arrived, both at home and at work, responsibilities and commitments start to fall away to the point where life starts to lack obvious purpose.

For many, there is an increasing amount of 'free time' that can be filled with more diverse leisure interests. They can explore activities that they always wanted to do. They take holidays on cruise ships, they tour in campervans, and they start going out to the movies again. In short, they find that at last they have the opportunity to soak up what life has to offer and they are thirsty for pleasurable experiences.

For others, this gradual sense of freedom becomes a time when they feel the need to get busy. As their parents age and their friends become ill, they become increasingly aware of the passing of time. They start to see time as a limited resource and they set broad plans for how they might spend their retirement years productively. A significant number of older people become involved in voluntary work, either at home or overseas. For them, there is usually an inherent cause or purpose behind the activity. There is a promise of great personal satisfaction when goals are ultimately achieved.

This is also the time of life when plans for small-business ventures are realised. Fulfilling a dream, developing an opportunity or diving into a long-planned project are all activities characterised by an underlying drive to achieve.

Many people gain satisfaction from acquiring new skills and learning new things during the retirement years. Although the arts and crafts scene can function simply as a pleasure, there is often an underlying agenda where the final product will bring lasting satisfaction to those involved. Quilt making, stained-glass work, and woodwork are examples of activities that are geared towards tangible achievement. We are proud of what we have made and we value the outcome.

There are few external factors or guides to determine how we should live in this rather unstructured phase of later life. There are no rights or wrongs. It is simply a matter of preference. However, it is important that we make active choices as to how we want to live. These years will slip by quickly, and as old age approaches, the opportunities to both enjoy life or to achieve in life start to dramatically reduce. Time will never seem so precious.

Stage 7: Old age

Finally, the time has arrived! However hard you have railed against it, old age now becomes a serious issue. We become less mobile, less aware and more dependent on others. Our focus tends to narrow and the goals that we set for ourselves draw closer to home and have increasingly shorter timeframes.

We learn to simply enjoy the flowers in our window box rather than delight in the complex garden that we might once have maintained. We feel pleased when we manage to walk to the mailbox instead of expecting to complete a 5-kilometre run every morning. Whether our preference is to focus on achievement or to focus on pleasure, the world seems to be steadily closing in on us in every way.

As a general rule, this is a time of life when we become more reflective and thoughtful. The 'doing' and the achieving starts to take a back seat and we become wiser and more accepting of the way things are. We have fewer expectations of ourselves or of others, and increasingly, we become detached observers of life as it goes on around us.

The 'wisdom' of old age is a very useful concept for us to explore further. A wise person is not necessarily proud of their achievements as such, but is simply mindful of their accumulated knowledge from past experience. It is not so much what we have achieved but what we now 'know' that is the key factor.

There is an inherent contentment and self-awareness in old age that no longer requires us to prove ourselves or to better ourselves. We are who we are, and we know ourselves pretty well. We no longer try to change ourselves or the world around us. We enjoy the simple pleasures again, and at the very end, we simply let go of life and drift away …

•

For some, the above review of life's stages might seem to be totally alien to your own view of how people live in the world. You might see the elderly as people struggling even more determinedly to achieve survival goals, rather than collectively becoming resigned to their mortality. Or you might see teenagers as individuals who are achieving new physical and intellectual skills every minute of every day, rather than just fooling around.

It may well be that we selectively attend to behaviours in others that reinforce our own particular view of the world. Or it may be that we choose to live in a sub-culture within society where our friends, family and colleagues all share our preference for either change or acceptance. We don't realise that it's not the only way to be and that we carry a bias in our worldview.

Whatever your opinion or your personal experience of the world to date, there is plenty to think about here. You can choose to take much greater responsibility in how you want to live your life. How do you really want the Pleasure/Achievement Principle to play out for you through the remaining stages of your life?

The following exercise provides a great opportunity to broadly review what your focus has been to date, and to consider how you would like it to be going forward.

Key memories

Having read the above review of the seven stages of life, consider your own life as it has been to date, and how you would like it to look in the future.

Firstly, jot down a few 'key memories' from each era in the table below. Don't think about it for too long, but just remind yourself of some of the events and places that you experienced.

Once you have done this, run your pen down the 'Pleasure' column and rate the degree to which your life at each stage has reflected the pursuit of pleasure. When you come to your current stage in life, continue on and project your future plans for enjoyment onto the stages yet to come.

Then repeat the exercise for the 'Achievement' column, rating the degree to which your life has involved the pursuit of goals and objectives. Again, try to project a lifestyle plan onto the stages yet to come.

Your Personal Life Stages	Key Memories	Degree of Pleasure (circle one)	Degree of Achievement (circle one)
Infancy		1 2 3 4 5 6 7	1 2 3 4 5 6 7
Childhood		1 2 3 4 5 6 7	1 2 3 4 5 6 7
Teenage Years		1 2 3 4 5 6 7	1 2 3 4 5 6 7
Young Adulthood		1 2 3 4 5 6 7	1 2 3 4 5 6 7
Mid-life Plateau		1 2 3 4 5 6 7	1 2 3 4 5 6 7
Later Adult Life		1 2 3 4 5 6 7	1 2 3 4 5 6 7
Old Age		1 2 3 4 5 6 7	1 2 3 4 5 6 7

Question 1

What patterns do you notice in the above exercise? What feels good about the ratings that you see?

Question 2

What are the key learnings or insights that you have gained from this exercise? Are there any changes that you would like to make in your life going forward?

Pleasure, achievement and the social environment

As well as considering how the Pleasure/Achievement Principle can play out over the history of our lives, it is also important to consider how factors in our current social environments can shape our lifestyle.

Three different levels of environmental influence will be considered below. We will review the potential influence of our culture, of our social networks, and of our family. At each level, we will find strong determinants that shape our worldview. Our psychosocial environment will shape our values, our perceptions, and the norms for our attitudes and behaviours.

Within different cultures, social groups and families, there will always be a varying degree of emphasis on either pleasure or achievement.

Cultural factors

The concept of culture is extremely diffuse and is often hard to define. Essentially, it describes a broad set of agreed principles that binds a group of people together. A culture usually has a well-defined membership (who's in and who's not). It also has well-defined roles within it and an agreed set of operating values. Most commonly, we think of culture in terms of geographic or ethnic groups.

Different cultures display different attitudes with respect to the Pleasure/Achievement Principle. For example, the Trojans were admired historically for their achievement orientation. They valued hard work ('to work like a Trojan'). Like most warlike or empire-building cultures, they tended to carry an achievement focus, striving towards specified goals. They were out to 'build' empires or 'win' wars. A Trojan soldier built his life upon an unrelenting determination to succeed and achieve. It was a satisfying, if somewhat unpleasant, way of life.

Conversely, other cultures were well known for their love of pleasure or 'the good life'. Hedonists, of course, are well known for their philosophical approach that argues for pleasure being the only intrinsic good. Their name derived from the Greek word meaning 'delight', and Hedonists valued the experience of pleasure above all other emotions. Their lifestyle was characterised by the continual pursuit of pleasure.

It is also interesting to note that even in the most warlike of castles during the Middle Ages, clever kings valued the presence of a court jester as a way to counterbalance the overbearing achievement orientation of the assembled knights!

Three fundamental ingredients for having a good time!

In the 1960s, the Hippy movement for many was characterised by the pursuit of pleasure. Life was all about 'sex, drugs, rock 'n' roll'. Interestingly, this holy trinity of indulgences has its historical precedent when Ancient Rome morphed from being the centre of an intensely focused military culture into an indulgent party town. The predominant social preoccupation for Roman citizens at this stage was characterised by 'wine, women and song'. Clearly, a heady mixture of sexuality, intoxication and music seems to be the time-honoured formula for having a good time!

Stereotypes used to characterise the personality traits of different nationalities will often make reference to the pleasure/achievement dynamic. As an example, Germans are generally renowned for their hard-working and structured approach to life, while the Caribbean countries are more often characterised by their 'laid-back' and easy-going approach.

Climate will obviously play a part, but overall, it is the inherent cultural values that influence our individual behavioural patterns and our collective lifestyles. Different countries value pleasure and achievement to varying degrees. And while, clearly, there is a huge degree of overlap and such generalisations can often become more than a little prejudicial in their expression, there is no denying that we can all be hugely influenced by our cultural norms, which then set the overall tone for our attitude.

Question 1

What is the predominant value expressed by your ethnic group?
Are you characterised as a happy or a determined culture?

Question 2

Does your culture primarily encourage:
a) the celebration of common traits, or
b) the pursuit of a mutual goal?

Societal factors

When we start to look more closely at the sub-groups within a culture, the situation becomes more interesting. The inherent values of sub-groups in society can quite clearly shape the members' tendencies towards pleasure or achievement.

Some social networks are focused largely on 'getting ahead' or making progress towards a specified goal. The group members will tend to make things happen rather than sit around. The topics of conversation at social gatherings will tend to be about recent successes and plans for future success.

Similarly, work teams or community task forces will invariably have defined outcomes to work towards. The bottom line is often about achieving specific goals. Only passing reference is ever made to having 'fun' in these types of work groups and social bonding is almost incidental. The members tend to view pleasure seeking as a rather lazy trait; such activities are largely seen as a waste of time.

Conversely, there are many groupings in society that celebrate the enjoyment of being together. Pubs, bars and coffee-morning groups gather simply to enjoy each other's company. Sometimes, a social gathering will have an explicit pleasure focus, such as a neighbourhood barbecue.

Many small town communities value their sense of connectedness and seem almost resistant to change. They do not wish to get bigger or to grow. The opportunity for development and growth would ruin the lifestyle that they already enjoy. These communities tend to value conservation and heritage. They are appreciative of life as it is rather than as it could be. Rather than getting ahead, they prefer to have a good time together rather than to try and make things happen.

In pleasure-oriented social groups, wry amusement is often expressed towards those who are always trying to get ahead and make a difference. Achievement-oriented people are seen as restless and driven, missing out on what the world around them has to offer. Hippies might have laughed at the stressed-out 'men in suits', but the businessmen often laughed at the lazy 'tree huggers'. In this way, members of the same culture became divided along a Pleasure/Achievement continuum.

It is of interest to note that many social organisations or groups specifically reference both pleasure *and* achievement in their charters. For example, most service clubs, such as Rotary or Lions, have a dual commitment to both community *service* and *fellowship*. Members are drawn together with a sense of common purpose, coupled with the pleasure of being together. In this way, a healthy balance is struck between the opposing values.

Similarly, most church groups will emphasise dual aspects of both 'being in a place of spiritual contentment' and 'striving to change oneself and the world for the better'. Spiritual contentment stands alongside self-improvement as the key lifestyle themes.

If an individual manages to access and balance both of these factors, then a state of fulfilment, as defined by the Pleasure/Achievement Lifestyle Matrix, will be the result.

Question 1
What is the predominant theme of the culture at your place of work? Is it comradeship or productivity?

Question 2
What are the primary values of your social group? Do they emphasise competitiveness and drive, or simply having fun and enjoying being together?

Question 3
Do people choose to live in your community primarily to get ahead, or are they living there because of the lifestyle?

Family factors
The socio-environmental influences that are strongest for us involve our family. The messages that our parents gave us throughout our childhood will be instrumental in shaping our worldview. Usually we take on board the messages that are given by the significant adults in our lives. However, sometimes we find that instead we rebel and experience a strong reaction against the values that our parents expressed. Either way, prevailing family values are strong determinants of the way we subsequently see the world.

As we saw earlier in the childhood section of the seven stages of life, parents often encourage their children in such a way that enormous pressure to succeed builds up. Individual pursuits such as swimming, ballet, horse riding and tennis are all activities where parents often push their children excessively. Exceedingly high performance standards are set.

These parents seem to almost live their own lives through the achievements of their children. Professional sport is littered with examples. A competitive attitude is encouraged and children are rarely allowed to relax. The standards that are set can become unrelenting and there is always another personal boundary for them to push towards. A driven, highly motivated attitude is the goal.

In other families, children are encouraged simply to be themselves. There is little pressure to be the best. Children are prompted to enjoy a range of life experiences. The emphasis is on appreciation and contentment. Children in these families learn to 'jump for joy' rather than to 'jump to beat their personal best'.

However, the nagging doubt for these children is that they may never reach their full potential. Although they are happy in their lives, they do not tend to experience the same degree of satisfaction and fulfilment that comes with having stretched oneself in order to achieve a valued goal. They may well underachieve and feel dissatisfied with their use of time.

Question 1

What did your parents encourage in your childhood? Were they pleased when you succeeded or when you were content?

Question 2

What was the most likely family motto for you as a child?

a) 'If at first you don't succeed, try, try and try again', or

b) 'Regardless of whether you win or lose, it's more important how you played the game'.

The physical environments that we create for ourselves

Just like the social environment, the physical environment is also an important determinant of how we live. Our immediate surroundings are not only an expression of our values, but they can also influence our lifestyle.

At work

For many years, when showing clients into my professional office, they would remark on the nice soft furnishings in the room. They would remark on the artwork, the décor and the cosy open fireplace. I would say in response that I was pleased to be able to offer a relaxing place for my clients to come to. Indeed, a feature of most clinical psychologists in private practice is that they enjoy the comfort of their surroundings!

However, I also realised that a counselling hour was not meant to be simply a pleasurable experience. It was obviously not enough to just provide clients with an enjoyable chat with a nice young man in a comfortable room. Although the room would often be seen by clients as an oasis of calm, away from the rigours of an otherwise stressful life, it was more important for them that my office served as a place of personal growth and change.

Primarily, there should be a clear sense of purpose to our conversations. Something should always be *achieved* before the end of each session, and it was important that some useful 'work' had been done.

The room did not have to seem like a factory or a workshop, but the bookshelves, the filing cabinet and the tidy desk needed to imply an organised, purposeful approach. This was meant to be a professional office after all, not a cruisy lounge. The clients were visiting a consultant, not a friend, and the physical environment needed to encourage an achievement orientation.

If your workplace is a workshop, then it is equally important to maintain a sense of orderliness and purpose. If the workbench is littered with half-finished projects from the weekend or still shows evidence of the previous Friday night drinks session, then it sets the wrong tone. Similarly, informative, useful charts and graphs look better on the wall than too many pictures. We are there primarily to achieve rather than to be indulged.

It is clearly important that, whatever job we do, we strike that fine balance between functional purpose and comfort in our work environment. And the primary emphasis needs to focus on an achievement orientation.

At home

In a house, every room is required to provide differing degrees of functionality and comfort.

Obviously, the kitchen and laundry are places where we have clear goals to 'achieve'. Meals get cooked, dishes get washed and ironing gets folded. The environment needs to reflect and encourage purposeful activity.

Conversely, the bedroom and lounge are places where we like to relax and enjoy ourselves. The theme is one of 'pleasure'. The colours are softer, the tone is calmer and we are invited to become more indulgent.

Other rooms are more ambiguous. The spare room can easily become 'the chill-out space' or 'the games room' where the family has fun, but alternatively it can become 'the office' or 'the sewing room' and a different character evolves.

Interestingly, the bathroom décor tells us a lot about our tendency towards pleasure or achievement. Essentially, it is a functional and purposeful room, but we can choose to transform it into a sensual experience by lighting candles, burning incense and running ourselves a warm relaxing bath with essential oils and bubbles. But how often do we make time for ourselves to do this or anything like it?

Where do you mostly tend to spend your time at home?
a) in the kitchen and laundry, or
b) in the lounge and bedroom.

As a final comment, it's worth noting that the famous interior designer William Morris (1834–96), once said, 'Have nothing in your house that you do not know to be useful, or that you do not believe to be beautiful.' Once again, the pleasure/achievement issue is seen to rear up, even within a classic Victorian statement about house furnishings!

In the garden

Vegetables to eat or flowers to enjoy … it can be as simple as that!

Many of us live with a small patch of land attached to our house that is ours to use as we wish. For those who take up the opportunity to be in the garden, it is an interesting mixture of opportunities for pleasure and satisfaction. Invariably, the garden requires a huge amount of input and it can feel like hard work. We weed, we water, we plant and we prune. There are compost heaps to turn, lawns to mow and rubbish to burn. You turn your back for a minute and the list of jobs to do has doubled. The garden never sleeps.

But among this sea of tasks, it is important to take the time to step back and enjoy the place that you've created and maintain. Often, this only occurs when like-minded visitors arrive and you show them around. You notice and point out the colours, the beauty and the freshness of the natural world. But shouldn't this happen even when you are spending time in the garden on your own? We tend to become overwhelmingly task oriented, but could easily take more time to enjoy and appreciate the natural environment around us.

A great 'bridging task' that sits astride both pleasure and achievement in the garden is for us to water the plants. As one waves the garden hose around, it is a good opportunity to deliberately spend some time just reflecting on the beauty and enjoying the moment. Never say, 'I've *got* to water the garden' but instead always say, 'I *want* to water the garden', and make sure that you define it as a pleasurable experience for yourself. (Remember the pleasure-oriented cognitive style that was described in Chapter Three.)

Key points to take from this chapter

- We have looked at how the Pleasure/Achievement Principle might play out over the course of a lifetime. *Seven stages of life* have been described. It can be seen that at different times, different issues tend to emerge. While no generic rules can be drawn up, it is clear that we need to address the challenges of each stage as they arrive.

- We have also looked at the *psychosocial environmental influences* that can shape our views. At all three levels of culture, social network and family, we can see that our worldview is shaped in part by the pervasive attitude that is held by others. We are encouraged to see the world through either a purposeful, goal-directed lens or else through a more appreciative, accepting lens. Each level clearly has a strong influence on us, and emphasises the importance of either pleasure or achievement in our lives.

- Finally, we have considered how the *physical environment* can influence the way that we live. Design features at home, at work and in the garden can all influence our lifestyle, and they serve to reinforce the messages that underpin the way we live our lives.

- We usually try to create physical environments that are appropriate to the lives that we choose to lead. We need to choose well and, overall, we need to aim for a healthy balance of themes.

Chapter Five
WHAT IS PLEASURE?

For people who value pleasure, it is the experience of special moments that make life worth living. They remember the good times, they seek out fun times, and they soak up the world through their senses. They value what is around them and are appreciative of the present. They enjoy being comfortable and content.

Those with a pleasure orientation look to surround themselves with positive stimulation. They love to consume the experiences that life has to offer. They soak up experiences such as music, scenery, tastes and colours. They love to feel the warmth of the sun on their skin.

They appreciate beauty, and they enjoy 'just being alive'.

Happiness defined as pleasure

'How simple and frugal a thing is Happiness: a glass of wine, a roast chestnut, a wretched little brazier, the sound of the sea. All that is required to feel happiness is a simple, frugal heart.' — Nikos Kazantzakis, *Zorba the Greek* (1946)

The role of pleasure in our lives

A sense of pleasure is central to a sense of feeling vital and alive. Feeling happy in the moment is an important quality to living well. We need to take time to smell the roses and to value the richness of the world around us.

We are always being encouraged to move forward, but it is also important to take time to enjoy being where we are. We should take time to relax, to notice and to enjoy the little things. We only live this life once and we should make sure that we appreciate and savour experiences to the full.

Emotions associated with a pleasure orientation

Positive emotions: joy, happiness, fun, laughter, contentment, calmness and peace.

Negative emotions: boredom, disillusionment, flatness and disappointment.

Life according to Murray

My dear friend Murray was lying in a hospital bed. He lived happily in a small rural community and was content to live quietly among family and friends. He had never seriously pursued a career. A couple of years ago, Murray had been diagnosed with cancer and doctors told him that his condition was inoperable. He now had only months to live. When I visited him, Murray looked at me with a quiet vulnerability and asked, 'Chris, you're the psychologist. How the hell am I going to handle this news?'

I had no idea what to advise, but I found myself saying the first thing that popped into my head: 'Murray, you have to set goals. You have to get to the end of the day, to the end of the week, and then get through to Christmas. Then we'll review your goals again.' Murray paused, then looked at me with a wry smile. 'Chris, to be honest, I've never set a goal for myself in my life! Do you really think that now, as I lie in a terminal cancer ward, is a sensible time for me to start?'

It was true! Murray's life had always been about living in the moment. Appreciating what was around him. He was always looking to be content, happy and accepting of circumstance. For Murray, whatever happened happened, even when facing death.

As he looked at life around him, he still felt good and he could still feel amused at all the ironic twists and turns that he saw. Murray would look back and remember all the fun he'd had. He was not concerned that he hadn't formally achieved a great deal in his life. Setting goals was never important to him.

For Murray, life was to be enjoyed for whatever had happened and for whatever unfolded before him. He loved to go with the flow, and wherever he went, he always carried a warm, contented smile.

He was the best kind of friend you could possibly have ...

Remembering feelings of pleasure

Sit and close your eyes. Make yourself comfortable and take time to recall the following images:

- Think back over your life and remember the times that you felt really happy. Perhaps it was the birth of a child. Or receiving a wonderful surprise. Or looking at a beautiful sunset.
- Now try to recall the times that were fun. Perhaps you were laughing helplessly with good friends. Perhaps you were playing on the lawn with a pet dog.
- Finally, remember feeling relaxed. Perhaps you were lying on a beach. Or lying in the long grass on a warm summer's day. Feel the warmth of the sun on your body. Relax.

These are examples of the moments that we should treasure. They are the moments that bring quality to our lives.

When the search for pleasure becomes excessive

An excess of pleasure quickly becomes unhealthy. We become 'indulgent'. There is no momentum to our lives, and we become increasingly sluggish and dissatisfied. Life as an endless party becomes meaningless, and we lack a sense of purpose. Fun can only last so long before we tire of it.

In the search for pleasure, we tend to consume more, we exercise less and we amuse ourselves increasingly with passive 'entertainment' such as television. We often look for new quick fixes to amuse ourselves, usually by seeking out even more indulgent experiences. We might drink more, spend more money or eat more chocolate. But, inevitably, these tactics only bring short-term relief from the tedium. All things in moderation!

To others looking on, an excessive focus on pleasure will seem to suggest that we have lost our way. It will seem that we are lacking in drive and purpose, and that we have let ourselves go. Our life will seem to have fallen out of balance. There will be no sense of satisfaction or pride in ourselves and we can seem weak willed.

'Life is just one huge fairground'

Becky (aged 21) loved life. She was always looking to have a good time. She rarely stuck at anything and had repeatedly dropped out of her college studies. Her parents were despairing about how to turn her life around and they were now funding therapy to help her settle down.

She had fallen into many classic scrapes during her teenage years and always lived life on the edge. She was the first up to party every time! There was a constant theme of impulsive decision-making and over-indulgence in her life.

In our first session she told me:

'The trouble with me is that I choose to spend all my time in the fun fair of life. Worse than that, I usually take the wildest of roller-coaster rides while I'm in there! I can spend all day having fun, and I'll even sneak back into the park again after the gates are closed!'

Clearly, Becky needed to spend a lot less time in 'the playground' and instead start to explore more rewarding and satisfying experiences farther down life's 'main highway'. It was her choice to make. She was literally spinning without direction. She carried high energy but no forward momentum. Her life was all about pleasure with no reference whatsoever to the deeper satisfaction of personal achievement.

Suddenly, Becky's issues had become crystal clear for her. She now realised exactly what she needed to do to feel a greater sense of fulfilment in her life.

An excessive pleasure orientation can seem superficial and pointless. In the end, we start to question whether having a good time matters so much. Surely, there is more to life than this? While we are alive, shouldn't we be trying to achieve something and make a difference?

When pleasure is missing

For many people, there is a distinct lack of pleasure in their lives. For some, it is simply that they don't know how to look for pleasure. They learned to adopt a negative worldview that doesn't allow for enjoyment. They have never learned to laugh and they carry a perpetually pessimistic outlook that only experiences relief when bad things don't happen. They are serious, dull and often seem to be going through the motions. They seem flat.

Often, they are diagnosed as depressed.

Swimming with dolphins

Linda (aged 40) could never relax. She worried about everything and had also been diagnosed as depressed. She lived alone and felt vulnerable. She had learned early in her childhood that if she relaxed, something bad might happen.

She always tried to avoid upsets and to guess what the 'right thing' to do might be. She was always trying to get it right for others and, as a result, she didn't know what she wanted for herself.

Linda hardly knew what pleasure was. Most of the time, she simply felt closed down and numb. She felt unwanted and useless. Her days were usually spent waiting for the next visit from her community nurse. If she was left alone, she would slowly stop eating and just stare at the walls. Medication didn't seem to help and her worries about potential side effects only compounded her problems.

I saw Linda for many years, repeatedly inviting her to set small weekly goals for herself. She planned to visit the local community drop-in centre or to bake a cake. Her occupational therapist would reinforce these simple goals and also helped her to organise her shopping and practical household chores. But more importantly, I also tried to schedule more *pleasurable* activities into Linda's life. To go to an afternoon movie. To schedule time to play with her cat. Or to run a scented bubble bath for herself. The goal-setting theme extended slowly over many months.

The wonderful jewel in Linda's crown of achievements finally occurred one summer when she forced herself to take a short holiday on a tour bus. While she was away I received a brilliant postcard from her:

'Chris, I've been out on the boat trip to watch the whales, just as we'd planned. But on the way back to shore, we saw a pod of dolphins and all impulsively went for a swim with them! It felt great! It was pure joy. It felt like "Heaven on Earth!" '

Her exuberance shone through her words. Linda had come from a very difficult place, but she had managed to create an exquisitely pleasurable experience for herself that many of us have yet to enjoy.

We all need to stay open to the possibilities for experiencing pleasure, and then simply allow those opportunities to unfold. Swimming with dolphins is a pretty pointless exercise but it is nevertheless an activity that for many captures the essence of a life well lived.

Other people can lose their experience of pleasure because they are excessively focused on achievement. Everywhere they look, they see things to do or mountains to climb. They are always doing what they *should, ought to* or *must*, rather than what they *want* to do. Their worldview is one of mild dissatisfaction with how things are. They feel that complacency is the main enemy in life, to be avoided at all costs. They do not allow themselves to relax and enjoy 'just being'.

At work, they experience a sea of demands to be met; while at home, there is also a list of things to do that never seems to end. Going to bed at the end of the day is not a pleasure but simply a relief from the demands of the world.

'An ambitious man is rarely content.' — Anon.

Some folk tend to run like crazy just to keep ahead of the task lists that they set for themselves. They become stressed. Others just give up and let the world wash over them, and become very gloomy indeed. Problems such as burnout or mental exhaustion often represent the end result of such a process. Their friends will tell them to slow down, relax and be more appreciative of simple things.

An excessive achievement focus often creates blind spots with regard to the experience of pleasure. We become so busy that there is little or no time to enjoy or celebrate simply being alive. We don't see or create the opportunities for ourselves.

Strengthening a pleasure orientation

Usually, an absence of pleasure means that we are under-stimulated, and that we do not have enough opportunity to enjoy ourselves. Depression is an obvious situation where people feel that there is no pleasure in their lives.

The immediate task is to identify pleasurable opportunities that could be scheduled and to ensure that they are experienced every day. The Pleasant Events Schedule is a 400-item list drawn up in the early 1970s by two clinical research psychologists, P.M. Lewinsohn and D.J. MacPhillamy, that includes a range of activities such as 'kicking through autumn leaves' and 'stroking the cat'. It provides a menu of options and is a good place to start when looking for pleasure. All the activities listed are free, healthy and enjoyable. This list of pleasant activities has remained centre stage over the subsequent 40 years, and is used particularly in treating depression and in promoting positive daily activities in the elderly.

Another exercise to elicit potentially enjoyable activities is a simple list of 'My Favourite Things', which is often used in mental health day programs to encourage a more enjoyable lifestyle. Several prompts are used to identify pleasurable activities and the items require us to focus on what we enjoy.

They invite us to consider those experiences that have given us pleasure in the past and that should be remembered as a means of providing pleasure in the future.

My favourite things
1. To do on a rainy day ...
2. To do on a sunny day ...
3. When I'm at work or helping others ...
4. With an animal or pet ...
5. With my family or a friend ...
6. Things that make me laugh most are ...
7. My favourite place is ...
8. My favourite topic of conversation is ...
9. My favourite fun thing to do ...
10. My secret indulgence or treat is to ...

When pressured, stressed or bored, we can easily fall into a state where we only see the blocks and barriers to enjoyment. There never seems to be enough time or opportunity for us to relax. There are always reasons not to bother.

If we are not careful, we tend to lose our connection to good experiences and we forget how easy it is to feel positive. The 'My Favourite Things' list allows us to remember what we enjoy, and it allows us to connect with those simple experiences again.

Scheduling more pleasurable activities into your life
Having considered the 'My Favourite Things' list, it's now time to commit to spending more time prioritising pleasure and ensuring that you make some time to engage in enjoyable activity.
  1. Choose one five-minute activity that you could enjoy shortly after arriving home each day.

2. Establish a 'special place' that is yours, and for pleasure only. It could be a park bench, a tree or a coffee bar. Go there regularly!

3. Choose one aspect of your work that you could develop into more of a fun activity. For example, you could send out at least one fun or pleasurable email/letter to a friend every day. Or run a teasing 'predictions site' for yourself regarding the likelihood of certain things happening. On opening your mail, always leave the pleasurable messages to open until last. Allow yourself time to be appreciative of the moment.

4. Choose one pleasurable activity or interest that you have either let slip or thought about but never bothered to take up. Schedule time to pursue this interest. Also, make sure that, every weekend, you arrange time specifically to relax and feel good.

5. Contact a friend whom you haven't seen recently, and reconnect over a coffee or by phone. Arrange to do something fun together, such as watching a movie, seeing a play or simply going for a walk.

6. Discuss with your family what they feel would be quality time for you all to share. This discussion will invariably generate a range of innovative suggestions. Be open to whatever suggestions emerge.

Apart from lacking a general awareness of opportunities for pleasure, we can also neglect our pleasure orientation by keeping an excessive focus on achievement. The more that we strive to achieve, the more we lose sight of the importance of appreciating the quality of the moment. We are always looking ahead, pushing through the inclination to accept the status quo, and we drive ourselves to challenge complacency.

For goal-oriented achievers, it can almost become a perceived weakness to enjoy the moment. The fear is that we will lose our motivation if we pause too long to appreciate the world. These are the folk who, when out for a walk, don't like to look at the view for long. Instead, they like to get going again as soon as they can. They seem impatient.

If you feel that you carry a strong preference for achievement, then it might just be that you need to deliberately schedule periods of 'down time' for yourself to be appreciative. Cups of tea while gardening, phoning a friend at morning tea, or standing outside to take a few deep breaths and to gaze at the sky … these small *micro-breaks* can be wonderfully energising and give us renewed vigour with which to address the day.

In our busy lives, we often forget the importance of letting go and relaxing. Pausing to reflect can seem like such a waste of time and is generally undervalued. Typically, people struggle to formally list what their relaxing hobbies or leisure activities might be. Since the advent of television and computer games, we tend to slump passively before a screen and simply allow technological stimulation to wash over us.

We often say that we *enjoy* TV, but the majority of time spent watching a screen simply results in a dull, brain-numbing state where the awareness of real-life experience is suspended. TV is high on the list of 'unhealthy pleasures'. Here, we cocoon ourselves with a warm glow of self-soothing, but we diminish the sense of feeling alive.

Authentic, real-life pleasure is usually to be found in natural experiences, such as watching waves on a beach, laughing with a friend or feeling the warmth of the sun on your face.

Opportunities for healthy pleasure abound. If we are truly mindful of our surroundings, then we can find enjoyment everywhere. More than anything, enjoyment is a state of mind.

Openness, clarity, sensitivity

I came across this delightfully simple idea many years ago, and it has stayed with me ever since. It is the title of a very readable book on Buddhist philosophy by Michael Hookham (see bibliography for details). The three concepts come from the ancient Buddhist tradition of accepting the world as it is, and they teach us how to *be* 'in the moment'.

Firstly, we need to be *open* to the whole range of stimulation that the world has to offer. Secondly, we need to ensure that we view the world *clearly*. Finally, we need to respond with *sensitivity*.

This is the essence of how to be fully present in the world, and of how to access pleasure.

Reducing an excessive pleasure orientation

When a pleasure orientation becomes excessive, then we need to seriously consider techniques for bringing our lives under better control. Over-indulgence in pleasure usually leads to clearly observable problems, such as excessive weight, financial difficulties or poor timekeeping. We value our enjoyment of the moment so much that we fail to keep good boundaries around our behaviour. We lapse into an indulgent pool of enjoyable excesses that slowly becomes toxic for us and those around us. Too much chocolate, too much alcohol or too much time on the couch, all become physical or mental health issues in the end.

Apart from the clinical problems of excess, for many of us, an overvalued pleasure orientation usually has more subtle consequences. For example, we might tend to *procrastinate*. We will hang on that little bit longer at a party or at the beach, and only leave when everyone else has gone home or the temperature drops. We might also 'treat' ourselves by watching just one more TV program, or deciding to play just one more game on the computer, before we do the dishes.

If it feels good, then you may ask, 'Why stop?' This is a very common message that we give ourselves, but the answer is that we lose a lot of valuable time as a result. Soaking in the bath, listening to music or lying in bed are all activities that are hard to bring to a natural conclusion. There is no natural endpoint. But there is a law of diminishing returns that kicks in. After a certain period of time, there is little extra to be gained from continuing the indulgence. It is usually best to 'time limit' pleasure and then move on to something else.

Bad habits can also involve very quick, opportunistic pleasures. We might develop a pattern of sneaking tidbits of food as we prepare a meal. Or we develop a habit of visiting the fridge before going to bed. It's easy to buy a chocolate bar as we pay for our petrol. These little guilty pleasures can quickly evolve into established habits and eventually erode our sense of self-control. We 'give in' to pleasurable urges. We rationalise and justify our actions, and minimise the significance of what we are doing.

Almost everyone has little patterns to their lives that involve sneaking 'treats'. Sometimes, these need to be nipped in the bud. While it would be draconian to deny ourselves any pleasure at all, we can all benefit from a regular review of our habits and choose to set clearer boundaries around them.

The general message to give to ourselves around excessive pleasure should be to *tighten up*.

Question 1

Think about one pleasurable activity that takes up too much of your time. How could you put more appropriate time limits around this behaviour? How can you draw the experience to a natural conclusion?

Question 2

Think about one small indulgent habit that you routinely allow yourself that feels wrong. What behaviour can you substitute instead? How can you achieve self-control in this area?

The satisfaction that comes from self-control

Self-control is the key concept in challenging excessive pleasure. Our cognitive focus needs to shift in order to allow us to focus on the longer-term benefits of self-control over the short-term pleasure of indulgence.

Whatever the indulgent behaviour, the short-term pleasure of the moment is invariably outweighed by more diffuse longer-term negative consequences to health, self-confidence and lifestyle.

The same dynamic applies to more disturbing habits such as lying or stealing. (Hopefully this will be of only passing interest to readers, rather than a pressing personal lifestyle concern!) Again the short-term benefits of dishonesty ('getting away with it') are far outweighed by the longer-term negative effects such as a lack of trust ('If I can do it, so will they') or a low sense of personal self-worth.

If you have stolen an ornament, then it will have a lesser value for you than something that you worked hard to acquire honestly. Similarly, if you pretend that you did something when you didn't then you are living a lie, with all the hollow emptiness that follows on from that. Some people may feel a smug pleasure from telling a lie, but they will feel no genuine pride or sense of personal authenticity. There is no real sense of satisfaction for them beyond the excitable but superficial buzz that so often drives dishonest behaviour.

In order to successfully manage an excessive pleasure orientation, we need to:

1) set clear behavioural limits for ourselves, and

2) learn to value the longer-term benefits of self-control.

Although these may initially seem diffuse and vague, an increased focus on pride, self-management and a sense of personal integrity are all great outcomes from bothering to take matters in hand.

As a final word about self-control, it is often tempting to set personal goals that emphasise restraint. These goals tend to be stated as negative outcomes, such as 'I won't buy chocolate any more.' (Dr Russ Harris, in his book *The Happiness Trap*, describes these as 'Dead Man's Goals', where a dead man can probably do better than you!) Instead of this, we should commit to a positive, life-affirming goal, such as to buy more fruit.

Emphasise what you are going to do more of, rather than what you are going to try not to do. As a result, your focus will subtly shift away from the indulgent activity towards a healthier alternative.

Key points to take from this chapter

- We looked at the nature of pleasure. We have seen that it has a vital part to play in our experience of life, and has an important qualitative function. For many, the experience of pleasure is the essence of living life well.

- We saw how pleasure is often lacking in people's lives and, in this situation, how people need to deliberately set goals and create opportunities to become more appreciative of life once again.

- We have also seen how an excessive achievement focus can distract us from pleasure, such that our constant striving for change does not allow us time to enjoy the moment. Several simple exercises were offered to help address this situation and bring more balance into the equation.

- We looked at how an excessive pleasure focus can lead to problems. We noted the value of good boundaries around our behaviour and the importance of exercising self-control.

- We do not need to go looking for pleasure. The opportunities to enjoy life are already all around us if we choose to be open and sensitive to them. If we stay mindful of the importance of a happy smile, then we are well on the way to living a fulfilling life.

Of Lily Pads and Stepping Stones

As we negotiate the river of life, with all its many moods and temperaments, we will inevitably find ourselves drawn to places that suit our own character.

For some of us, it is the surging rapids and turbulent waterfalls that excite and delight. These folk enjoy striding purposefully and energetically across 'the stepping stones to success'. For them, life is a challenge to be savoured.

Others are drawn to the quieter and more reflective backwaters that provide calm and soothing opportunities to relax. They soak in luxurious pools. They enjoy dancing lightly and happily on 'the lily pads of pleasure'. For them, life is beautiful and a true wonder to behold.

Where are you at this time of your life? Surging along in the rapids trying to get ahead, or dreamily floating around in a pool of tranquillity as life rushes past somewhere else?

Is this how it's always been for you?

Is this how you want it to stay?

In the end, the choice is yours ... an exciting, turbulent world of stepping stones, or a more peaceful, gentle world of water lilies? Wherever you may be in your life, you can always choose what your next step might be ...

Chapter Six
WHAT IS ACHIEVEMENT?

For those who value achievement, the central theme is to make positive changes in their lives. They love to have energy and drive. They focus on getting things done and they try to make a difference. With this perspective, life is more about 'doing' things than just 'being'.

An achievement orientation means we are always looking to change the world around us. We also value self-improvement and are always seeking to learn more. There is a sense of discipline and purpose associated with an achievement orientation.

A key principle is to *set goals* and drive towards them. We focus on outcomes. Rather than seeing the world for the way that it is, we are always planning for change. We like to see tangible outcomes for units of time spent, and we enjoy the effort of getting there. When required, we can dig deep. We are motivated and committed to seeing a project through to its final conclusion.

We like to look back over the day and feel *satisfied* with what we have done. We like to know that we have gained something from the day. Even if we are simply looking at a pile of folded washing or a clean bathroom, we know that it has been a day well spent. We have achieved something.

Our heroes tend to be those who have climbed mountains, won sporting glory or made a lot of money. We admire great leaders and, overall, we strongly value *success*.

Happiness defined as satisfaction

'Many persons have the wrong idea about what constitutes happiness. It is not attained through self-gratification but through fidelity to a worthy purpose.' — Helen Keller, *The Simplest Way to be Happy* (1933)

The role of achievement in our lives

The drive to achieve plays a hugely important role in our lives. Without a sense of purpose, our lives lack meaning. From the moment that we get up, we are starting to achieve. We plan our day, we make lists and we become energised. More importantly, *achievement is the key concept that underpins self-esteem*. We develop a strong sense of self-confidence as a consequence of achievement. However much we might experience pleasure, we will never generate the depth of self-belief that derives from having successfully achieved.

Emotions associated with an achievement orientation

Positive emotions: pride, satisfaction, courage, enthusiasm, motivation and drive.

Negative emotions: tension, frustration, irritability, restlessness, impatience, disappointment and failure.

Life according to Craig

My colleague Craig was an amazingly successful businessman. He knew power, wealth and status. He was paying for our meal in the most expensive restaurant in town. As we ate, he asked me how things were going.

'All's going well, Craig. I've got so many options that I'm almost spoilt for choice as to what to do next with my life.'

'Well, Chris, don't forget that options have value. You can sell options. When I was a boy and I saw a queue, I'd stand in it. By the time I was close to the front, I knew that I had something to sell. Out of nothing, I'd created something that had value. It was an option that I could then sell.'

For Craig, there were opportunities to create value everywhere that he looked. Even standing still, he could achieve something!

Connecting with feelings of satisfaction

Sit down and close your eyes. Make yourself comfortable and really take the time to recall the following images:

- Think back over your life and remember the times that you felt really proud. Perhaps you had passed an exam. Or you had won a competition. Or you had climbed a mountain.

- Now try and recall the times that were satisfying for you. Perhaps you had completed an assignment. Or you were sitting down after a long day in the garden.

- Finally, remember anticipating an opportunity that filled you with a positive enthusiasm to succeed. You could be standing at the start line for a race or waiting for a job interview.

- These are examples of the moments that we should treasure. They are the moments when we focus on what we have achieved or still could achieve.

Achieving high standards

Achievement is not just about getting things done; it is also about achieving to a set standard. This is where many achievement-oriented people find their greatest satisfaction. Standards of tidiness, hygiene and personal fitness are all examples of goals that individuals often set for themselves. The goal is to achieve a certain qualitative level in some aspect of one's life. For many, there is an inherent satisfaction in keeping a tidy garden or driving a well-polished car.

These are usually maintenance tasks that do not have a lasting outcome. We can only attain the goals so long as we continue to put in energy. However, the feelings of satisfaction and pride experienced on achieving and maintaining the standard are often hugely rewarding. It is important, however, to make sure that the standards do not become unreasonable, such that the effort required to succeed is not really worth the result.

The virtuous feelings of pride and satisfaction in attaining a set standard have lost their social significance in recent years. High standards are not universally valued. Nonetheless, self-esteem and self-confidence are still concepts that are underpinned by a sense of holding oneself to a satisfactory standard of both conduct and dress. Overall, it is still good to set standards for oneself, and this creates a stronger sense of positive self-regard.

Modern life encourages us to always be looking to get ahead and to achieve. Society values success and there is a competitive edge to most aspects of our world. As we have already seen, school teaches us to set goals and to strive for self-improvement. By and large, life for most of us is about getting things done.

Our goals are many and varied. Firstly, there are the basic daily tasks to accomplish, such as cooking, cleaning and shopping. Then there are more discretionary tasks to fulfil that are not so important but will improve the overall quality of our lives. These include activities such as redecorating the lounge or cleaning the car. Finally, there are challenging tasks that we set ourselves purely as a personal challenge, such as running a marathon or learning a new language.

In general, we can choose how long the list of daily tasks that we create for ourselves will be. We can define for ourselves what needs to be done. Our task list can include both tangible, objective goals — such as digging a ditch — or intangible, subjective goals, such as self-improvement.

Many personal goals will focus on intellectual achievement. For many of us, life is seen as a continuous learning opportunity and many people spend their lives enrolling in courses to gain further qualifications and awards. Although they are more abstract in nature, these goals play an important role in bringing fulfilment to our lives.

Goals can have a short-term focus, such as planning a shopping trip, or a long-term focus, such as planning for retirement. Either way, we are looking ahead and creating a vision of how we want things to be. We assume that our lives will be generally better for delivering on the plan.

When the search for achievement becomes excessive

When the search for achievement becomes excessive, we become discontented. We can never settle and we are always looking to improve. We can seem restless and agitated. The drive to get things done becomes overwhelming and we lose the ability to enjoy things simply as they are. Our relationships often suffer as a result. Even if our partners and friends are racing along at a similar pace to ourselves, it is hard to relate intimately to each other, as we are all focusing intently on the way ahead rather than on how well we are doing right now.

There never seems to be enough time when the drive to achieve becomes excessive. An achievement orientation requires us to keep our eye on the clock, and it is easy for time to become our enemy. We become pressured, over-committed and tense.

Not enough time to relax

Oliver liked living life in the fast lane. He was a snappy young lawyer who would often stay up until 3 a.m. preparing for court the next day. He worked hard and he played hard. My daughter knew him well.

He lived life to the full. He drove a red sports car, rode fast motorcycles and attended salsa dance classes. He was studying for a Masters degree too. He was always on the go.

However, Oliver also struggled to sleep. He seemed restless and easily distracted at times. He often used sleeping tablets, and in explaining why, he came up with the following memorable quote:

'I simply don't have the time to spend a whole hour in bed trying to doze off. It's far more efficient for me to just take a pill!'

For Oliver, relaxing in bed at the end of the day was a waste of time. He was acutely aware of the pressure of time and he couldn't stand to simply 'hang around', even in bed. He was classically 'driven' and was always looking ahead to the next opportunity in his life with great energy and enthusiasm.

The lovely thing about Oliver was that all his friends were drawn to his bubbly, irrepressible personality, and his colourful life somehow added brightness to theirs …

When achievement is missing

For some, life lacks any sense of purpose or forward movement. Since infancy, they seem to absorb life passively, rarely reaching out to try new things or to see what might be gained by a little more effort. They lack motivation to change and seem content to live life as they find it.

Others may find that through circumstance, such as restricted opportunities in life or childhood neglect, they have learned to simply accept life as it is. Essentially, they have given up on trying to achieve. They might have been set impossibly difficult targets in the past and the subsequent repeated failures have led to a sense of overwhelming helplessness. They will sometimes seem to *avoid* setting goals or challenges for themselves.

Another scenario is when the pleasure focus is excessive. In this case, the strong preference to have fun in the moment tends to overwhelm the individual's awareness of the importance of achievement. An excessive pleasure orientation generates an achievement blind spot, where we fail to recognise that we lack drive and ambition. We underachieve because we do not realise that we are!

Wayne's story

Wayne was brought to see me by his father Terry, who was extremely worried about his lack of motivation.

Wayne was 25, had never held down a job and was still living at home. He was always asleep when Terry went off to work, and when he came home nothing had been done around the house. The dishes were still in the sink and the curtains were still drawn.

Wayne would be cocooned in a sleeping bag in front of his PlayStation, cuddling a hot-water bottle and surrounded by piles of empty chip packets, chocolate wrappers and fizzy drinks.

'He tells me that he's happy, but he does nothing all day. Where's the satisfaction in that?' commented Terry.

Wayne was actually depressed, and like a lot of depressed people, he was trying to feel better by indulging in pleasure rather than getting on and achieving something. He was 'self-soothing'.

For Wayne, the challenge would be to connect with a sense of achievement, however small, and to look for an increased sense of satisfaction and pride in himself. He needed to set even the smallest of goals for himself.

He started by buying a packet of sunflower seeds …

For individuals who lack an achievement focus, the inevitable result is that towards the end of their lives they will usually feel that they have not achieved their full potential. Life may have been enjoyable enough, but somehow it will have lacked a sense of fulfilment. All the fun in the world cannot make up for a lack of genuine satisfaction with what has been actually achieved.

Strengthening an achievement orientation

There are several simple ways to strengthen an achievement orientation. The fundamental theme to every strategy is to identify and commit to clear *goals*. We need to know what we want to get out of the next hour, the rest of the day, the rest of the year, the next five years, and the rest of our lives.

Goal setting

Having set ourselves behavioural goals, we also need to develop the self-talk of an achievement orientation, where we value outcomes and feel proud.

All goals should be *SMART* goals. This acronym means: Specific, Measurable, Achievable, Realistic and Timely. SMART goals can be set across all three domains of one's life: at home, at work and in one's leisure pursuits. They can be short, medium or long term; objective or subjective; and they should always be life affirming.

Experienced goal setters will always ask, 'Does this add value to my life?' It's a great question. It ensures that we are always moving in a valued direction, and that we are setting goals that are healthy for us. We are enriching our lives.

> # Does it make the boat go faster?
>
> An interesting variant of the phrase 'Does it add value?' came from the New Zealand America's Cup sailing crew. Whatever decision they made about their team, from the supplies that were ordered to the training schedules that were designed, the key reference question was always: 'Does it make the boat go faster?'
>
> Immediately, we see that Team New Zealand had an intense focus on outcomes and goals, and strived for success over everything else. They usually won.

It is important to build both tangible and intangible goals into your life. By ensuring that you are always 'creating' and 'learning', you are remaining fresh and energised. There is always something else to explore further, and ultimately, an achievement focus encourages us to take any opportunity for development that we can see.

Setting purposeful goals

a) Tangible goals

Short-term: List one daily responsibility that you could add to your list that will feel satisfying once it's complete. Perhaps you could sweep the path, or fold the laundry. Note that it will rarely be a pleasurable activity, but it will be satisfying to see when it's complete.

Medium-term: Find one household project that you can start to attack. Perhaps you could reorganise the spare room or re-landscape the garden. Write down the intermediate steps involved.

Long-term: Think about what you would like to achieve over the next five years. Perhaps you would like to build yourself a boat or set up a craft shop. Develop a specific plan to get there, identifying the timelines and the intermediate steps required to get there.

b) Intangible goals

Short-term: Try to learn one new thing each day. For example, when you turn on your computer, experiment with a new function that you do not understand, before clicking on your emails or favourite websites. Look to create a 'learning stretch' for yourself.

Medium-term: On a weekly basis, set yourself a new goal. This could be to learn a new skill or to take a book from the library that broadens your knowledge. When you put it down, you should feel pleased that you have learned something new.

Long-term: Think about registering for a course or a training program that teaches you new skills. Your increased knowledge is an intangible outcome but one that makes you feel that the year has been worthwhile. You have learned something new, such as how to go flyfishing, or how to make jewellery.

Reducing an achievement orientation

When the drive to achieve gets out of hand, we sometimes need to learn to slow down and be more appreciative of life. Not every activity needs to be purposeful, and everyone needs a degree of 'down time' to relax and enjoy the moment. Wall-to-wall goal setting becomes unsustainable in the longer term.

In most sporting codes, there is a clear need to pace oneself and conserve energy. A boxer may wait out rounds four and five, and then explode into action in round six. A middle-distance runner might sit back for a lap, biding their time. Tennis players can unexpectedly drop games in the second set, saving themselves for the third.

In many tasks, we back off or slow down in the middle phase before the 'big push' at the end. Often, we can see surges of progress towards goals, and achievement is rarely the result of a linear accumulation of success.

While these down times cannot really be described as pleasurable, they are definitely times when the focus on speed, power or endurance has been overshadowed by a need to take stock, adjust expectations and get comfortable with the situation. It is rarely possible to maintain 100 per cent energy for 100 per cent of the time. Scheduling periods of energy maintenance to complement periods of intense drive is a key coaching skill in sport and produces optimum outcomes.

And so it is in life.

Scheduling breaks

We have talked earlier about using naturally occurring *micro-breaks* to reflect. Bus stops, coffee breaks, toilet stops and photocopier breakdowns all provide great opportunities to pause and calm down. Most of these incidents will seem inconvenient and frustrating blocks to progress, but if you are living in the moment, they are simply aspects of life to be experienced for what they are. They may not be what you had planned for, but they are reality, warts and all, and represent part of life's 'rich tapestry'.

But rather than wait for an inconvenient break to force you to reflect, why not schedule regular, deliberate breaks on the hour, in order to take stock and to breathe? Make a habit of noticing detail in the world around you and being more relaxed.

Achievement-oriented folk tend to lose sight of the world immediately around them. They are always looking ahead and planning for change. They rarely stop to notice or appreciate the beauty of the wood grain in a desktop or the wonder of a raindrop trickling down a window. Sometimes, they can even forget to appreciate the family photos on the wall …

In addition to micro-breaks, we need to ensure that we schedule time for more formal interests and hobbies. In effect, we need to *plan for our relaxation!* There are many inventories of pleasurable activities, but usually, it is simply a matter of prioritising pleasurable leisure activities over more urgent, demanding tasks.

It will always be difficult to decide whether to defrost the fridge or take a walk in the park. Both are important but non-essential activities. For some people, the walk will take an obvious priority, but for others, it is hard to do this while there is still a job to be done in the house.

Clearly, we need to make sure that we schedule adequate time for both.

You could write your own list of pleasurable activities — and make sure that you do something each weekend that you can later describe as enjoyable. Sometimes, it adds fun to write the activities on scraps of paper and put them in a jar. These activities could include doing a jigsaw, walking around the block, looking at old photos or cooking a new dessert. Pull out one crumpled idea each day and commit to actually doing it. You will be surprised at how the quality of your life improves by creating just a little more time that is dedicated to pleasure.

Developing an appreciation of the present

Learning to appreciate the present, regardless of the potential for change, is a difficult perspective to grasp for those with an excessive achievement orientation. It sounds dangerously like settling for second best or reduced standards. Learning to simply enjoy playing the game, rather than winning the game at all costs, is a scary concept to some of us!

Enjoying the process, rather than the outcome, requires a very different outlook. Phrases such as 'whatever happens will happen' or 'at least we tried' don't feel intuitively right to achievement-focused individuals.

The ability to accept disappointing outcomes feels weak. 'I didn't get where I am by accepting disappointing outcomes!' they might say … However, for pleasure-oriented individuals, accepting adverse outcomes is okay. They enjoy the journey, regardless of the destination. Wherever they end up, they can accept that it's just the way that events played out.

An appreciation of the present requires us to hold a balanced overview. We learn to see both sides of a story. We enjoy an evolving drama, regardless of the eventual outcome. We are passive but thoughtful observers of life, absorbing the bittersweet range of experiences on offer.

Coming last in a race is a curious, somewhat embarrassing experience, but it can later become the basis for an amusing, meaningful story that gives a powerful message. In a strange way, we are usually the richer for almost any experience that we have. Life is not just about winning. (Now seriously, are all you achievers with me on that point? It's important!)

The value of humour

Someone with an excessive achievement focus can easily lack humour. The pursuit of goals can become a serious affair and fun is often the first casualty. It can seem like an unnecessary, often irritating distraction. But humour has a function and the tension release associated with a good laugh is invariably good for us.

If we can laugh, then usually we know that we are in a good place.

Telling funny stories

Think of a funny story that you could tell about your past. Think of a time when you made a mistake. Or a time when an unexpected outcome gave a delightful twist to a best-laid plan. Think of a story where there was humour because outcomes were *not* achieved. A story with a humble message …

These are all stories about the way life actually is, regardless of how hard we strive for certain outcomes. Humour often requires us to accept an unfortunate turn of events but to enjoy the journey regardless of outcome. Humour is a great antidote to the stress of feeling pressured to achieve.

Learning to relax

Being able to relax is an important skill for those who lead a driven, goal-oriented life. When we relax, we are obliged to slow down, to let go and to lose ourselves in the moment. The full script of my own relaxation CD is provided in Appendix 2. This gives a detailed script for the muscle relaxation exercises, including the rationale for why we should learn to stay calm.

There are many CDs available offering relaxation techniques, but essentially, they all encourage the listener to slow down, breathe calmly, and induce a warm heavy feeling throughout the body. They usually take about twenty minutes to half an hour to complete.

The relaxation instructions basically suggest that we can let go of muscle tension. As we tense and relax muscle groups, we are encouraged to talk ourselves down into a deeper state of physical wellbeing. Our bodies will naturally tense up in response to danger or threat, but during relaxation, we encourage ourselves to let go and unwind. We allow ourselves to feel good.

Key points to take from this chapter

- We have looked at the role and function of an achievement orientation. Achievement brings purpose, meaning and momentum to our life. We feel more confident and self-affirmed for having achieved. The key emotion that derives from holding an achievement orientation is the feeling of satisfaction.
- Achievement requires us to set goals and to always look ahead. The goals that we set can be either tangible or intangible, and they can vary a great

deal in their timeframes. Some achievers hope to make a lasting difference to the world, while others simply aim for their own personal development. Sometimes, the achievement is simply to live life to a certain standard rather than to achieve an objective goal.

- We have reviewed the basic structure for a goal-setting approach that supports an achievement orientation, and have also looked at how we might balance an excessive drive with a more pleasure-oriented approach. A number of suggestions to enhance appreciation of the moment have been reviewed, including relaxation techniques.

- Overall, the energy and vitality of an achievement perspective is to be admired. It gets us out there and doing things. Achievers will usually look back on their lives with considerable satisfaction and pride, having completed a great deal and having made a significant difference in so many different ways.

- Without an ultimate sense of achievement, we simply cannot say that we have lived a fulfilling life.

Climbing the Path to Mount Fulfilment

As the path to Mount Fulfilment grows ever more demanding, we find ourselves increasingly tempted by our demons. Having left the sulphurous Pits of Stagnation far behind, we still have a long way to go. And as we trudge onwards, we remain vulnerable to losing sight of the path.

For some, the distractions of the Challenging Cliffs of Achievement will draw them aside, irresistibly keen to test themselves against the odds. They thrive on the danger, the excitement and the challenge of the place. Bristling with technological aids and with heads full of plans, they will think that they are in Heaven. They are drawn away from the path by the challenge and by the excitement, and they often lose their way.

For others, the distraction will be more seductive in nature. They will glimpse the warm steam rising gently from the Sensual Pools of Pleasure, and they will be drawn towards the opportunity to relax. They will close their eyes and soak up the experience with joy in their hearts. They too will feel that they have found Heaven. But they are wrong. The lure of the pools will have drawn them from the path, but they too will never achieve total fulfilment.

On either side of the path, there are many, many opportunities such as these for our *driven* or *indulgent* lifestyle biases to draw us away from the straight and narrow. The path is demanding enough as it is, and we cannot afford to become lost in prolonged side trips.

By all means explore a little as you go, but do beware the dangers of straying too far or for too long! Keep to the balanced path, and keep to a steady pace, and a life of fulfilment will eventually be yours to savour!

Chapter Seven
APPLYING THE PRINCIPLE TO YOUR LEISURE

When a clinical psychologist reviews a client's current situation, they imagine three segments of a pie chart that represents the client's time. Firstly, there is the time spent at *work*. Secondly, there is *domestic* time spent at home and with family. And thirdly, there is *leisure* time.

We will consider the leisure section first, because it is here that our natural preference for either pleasure or achievement plays out most clearly. It is usually easy to see our natural bias in our leisure pursuits, both in terms of what we do and how we do it.

In this busy world, it is often hard to find time for leisure. It can be embarrassing to be asked in a job interview what your hobbies and interests are. People will often refer to what they used to do rather than what they enjoy now. Work pressures, parenting duties and general domestic chores often mean that we have no time left for ourselves, and leisure time just gets squeezed out of our lives.

Ask a friend how they spent the weekend and their answer will probably fall into one of two categories. They will either say something like, 'It was great! I cleaned out the spare room and I mowed the lawns', or they will say, 'It was great! I caught up with some old friends and we took a walk on the beach.'

Neither answer is right. Neither is wrong. And of course, we can all get involved in a fair amount of both types of activity. But the key question is to ask ourselves where we place our emphasis along the spectrum of possible replies. More importantly, we need to consider whether we have an unhealthy bias and whether we should bring a greater balance to the way in which we spend our free time.

Leisure time is discretionary time and, as a result, it becomes something of a blank canvas for us to use as we wish. Upon waking on a Saturday morning, we have a choice. We can get up early and rip into a list of jobs to be done or we can roll over and have a lie-in. There are no work imperatives or social expectations to influence our decision.

The three types of leisure activity

Leisure activities are usually divided into three categories. To live healthy lives, we need to ensure that our leisure activities include *physical*, *social* and *creative* activity. Let us consider these three areas in turn, and decide how the Pleasure/Achievement Principle might play out in each.

Physical activity

This is the domain of leisure that really excites achievement-oriented individuals. They love to be active, to get their muscles pumping and to achieve personal goals. It often involves being competitive and striving towards satisfying outcomes. Gyms are full of people counting calories burned, kilograms lifted and minutes spent rowing. These people gravitate towards treadmills in a way that is almost incomprehensible to pleasure seekers. They strain and grunt their way towards satisfying targets, often transcending pain in their efforts to achieve.

In contrast, the more indulgent pleasure seekers find gentler ways to exercise and keep fit. They stroll on the beach, gently tend their garden or go for a leisurely cycle ride. Their focus is more in the moment and the sensory pleasure of the experience. The goal of improved fitness is almost accidental.

It is interesting to listen carefully as people describe the activities that they pursue. The language can be very different.

For some, golf is a social game where they can relax and enjoy a joke with friends. There are often cans of beer in the golf bag and they laugh if they miss the ball. For them, the golf course is a 'playground'. Mistakes are okay. Driving home from a game of golf will probably involve happy chuckles at silly situations that evolved and at stories that were told and will undoubtedly be re-told.

For others, playing golf is a more serious matter. They play to a handicap, they use the best gear they can afford, and they experience ecstatic triumphs and gut-wrenching failures as they grind out their rounds. They never laugh at themselves, and for them, the course is always 'a challenge'. They play against their opponents, their previous score and the course itself. It's all about winning. As they drive home, these folk might be carrying a deeper, quieter feeling of satisfaction and success, with the club's annual trophy sitting in the passenger seat beside them. But for every winner, there will be a loser driving home. The frustrated achiever who came second will be fluctuating between feelings of anger and despair, determined to dig deeper and do better next time. They are grappling with the flip side of an achievement orientation, with all the associated emotions of disappointment and failure.

If we go hiking in the great outdoors, the need to balance pleasure and achievement is usually quite clear. Walking some distance should always be a careful balance of making progress towards the next landmark, while also taking time to pause and admire the view along the way.

It is a sad character who goes out so hard that there is no opportunity to appreciate the scenery, but it is an equally sorrowful individual who simply dawdles along without any expectations or sense of progress towards the identified goal. Worse still, if they decide not to bother walking the whole track!

Physical activity necessarily involves muscles, which are the favourite part of the body for achievers. They love strength and power, and they like to feel toned. They love gyms and have target times, distances and weights to attain. In contrast, pleasure seekers do not like gyms and don't understand them. Their body tone is softer.

Achievers will go to the swimming pool determined to knock off 50 lengths before breakfast. Conversely, pleasure seekers only go to the pool occasionally and simply flap around and see if they can float on their backs. They usually only go after lunch because, for pleasure seekers, comfort is paramount.

Learning not to be a wimp!

Mr Pleasure was standing in the chilly water up to his knees. He was stuck, in the time-honoured tradition of a wimp at the beach trying to go for a swim. All around, fearless hunks of masculinity were wading past him and diving straight into the waves. But he was wavering and could not advance.

Suddenly, he realised it was his preference for comfort that was holding him back. He was warm and dry, and the sea was cold and wet. He was immobilised by his bias towards pleasure. But if he shifted his emphasis from 'keeping warm and dry' to instead focusing more on the objective of 'going for a swim', he would be able to plunge on in, have his swim, towel down, and subsequently feel really satisfied and even proud about his manliness.

Resolving to stay firmly goal focused, he dived forward gloriously, thrilling to the exhilaration of knowing that an achievement orientation had finally erupted into his life. He had overturned the embarrassments of a lifetime.

His life suddenly seemed so much stronger for having realised the change. Mr Pleasure had finally learned that, sometimes, an unswerving commitment to achievement is the key to resolving indecision, procrastination and self-doubt.

Social activity

Social activities obviously involve people, and what interests us here is whether the people we spend time with are adding value to our lives. Do our friends help us to 'get things done' or are they simply 'fun to be with'. When we review the people with whom we choose to spend our leisure time, it is usually to either engage in purposeful activities or else it's primarily to have fun and relax.

Purposeful social activities often occur when we join community organisations, fundraising groups, working groups and political action groups. Pleasure-oriented groups tend to be less structured and focus on activities such as going out for a meal, to the movies or to parties.

Speaking of parties, there are two very different scenarios that can play out at parties, depending on one's personal style.

Firstly, there are the upwardly mobile types who go to the 'right' parties, where they hope to meet the 'right' people and strengthen their social networks. They tend to socialise with colleagues or community contacts rather than friends. They go to achieve something. At a party, they will try to 'work the room' and 'leverage opportunity'. They have the annoying habit of looking over your shoulder to scan the room to see if there are more useful connections to be made. Once the party has been worked over, they take their leave in an organised and efficient way, achieving 'closure' to a productive evening. Business cards may have been distributed and arrangements made with key players to meet up later in the week. But somehow, it seems that the actual 'fun' of the party experience has just passed these people right on by …

In contrast, there are those people who really know how to party! For them, a party is an invitation to let down their hair. It's an opportunity to fool around, relax and have a heap of fun. They dance, they drink, they pop balloons and they stay there until there's no one left to party with. They flog themselves to exhaustion in an indulgent search for the biggest laughs, the craziest experiences and the best new friends. The following day, they usually wake up with a hangover, having achieved absolutely nothing at all. They often don't even know who they were partying with!

Pleasure seekers are usually left with a generalised feeling of disquiet that perhaps they could have managed themselves a little better, and they vaguely consider that they might try to carry themselves with a little more restraint next time. They never do. But in the meantime … they certainly know they've enjoyed one heck of a party!

We all need to strike a balance here. Parties are generally considered to be social playgrounds where entertainment is the main theme. But, like Hollywood, there is often another agenda to be considered, where our lives become richer for the contacts that we make. Besides the glitz, the glamour and the superficial fun, there are also informal conversations and connections to be made. Parties aren't just for fun. They're also potentially very useful places to be.

In summary, it's a good idea to try to leave every party with at least one new funny story to tell and also at least one new useful contact to explore. In essence, make sure that you always mix a little business with your pleasure when you're out and about!

Friends and rivals

If we carry a pleasure orientation, this sets us up with *best friends* whom we enjoy and with whom we love to party.

If we carry an achievement focus, this sets us up with *arch rivals* whom we respect and with whom we love to compete!

Creative activity

Creative activity means any activity that stretches you personally. Usually, this means learning a new skill or developing new knowledge. We can often find areas for personal development by simply listening to what we say. 'I'm no good at acting' or 'I'm no good at singing' suggests that we could join an amateur dramatic society or a choir, and see how good we can become!

We all tend to limit ourselves by our descriptions of what we can't do or what we don't like. This tends to be a 'black and white' analysis, however, and the real question should be to ask *to what extent* we can do things, or *to what extent* we like to do things.

In finding activities that provide for a personal stretch, we need to harness and develop our natural curiosity about the world. Curiosity is a wonderful attribute and allows us to flourish as we explore what the world has to offer.

For achievers, the search for a creative stretch will probably involve learning a new skill. They will extend from the comfort of the familiar and will look for a new activity or learning challenge. They will value the opportunity to explore new possibilities and different experiences in their life.

They will aim for consistently improved performance in their new chosen skill. They will probably take lessons, and they will compare their rate of learning against a benchmark. They may be learning a language, a practical skill or a new sport, but whatever interest they turn to, you can be assured that they will be trying hard to succeed.

For pleasure seekers, the tendency will be different. They will tend to seek out more reflective interests, where the quiet appreciation of a new sensory experience is valued. They may choose to visit art galleries or museums, where they can sit and appreciate beautiful things.

They may also try different ethnic foods, different styles of music or new yoga techniques. Overall, it is more of a passive personal stretch, qualitatively different from the more focused drive that characterises the creativity of an achiever.

Playing the guitar

If you were to stroll past a guitar, or perhaps a piano, would you be more likely to:

a) strum some familiar chords, or

b) try to learn a new tune?

There is a fine balance here between enjoying the comfort of the familiar and the satisfaction of acquiring new skills.

It is a good idea to ensure that we have a creative theme to our leisure activities. Whether we choose to learn new skills or simply to enjoy new sensations, our lives will certainly be the richer for the broader range of experiences that we will have as a result.

'Fishing isn't really about catching fish'

Shortly after a promotion at work, young Richie's new boss asked him to go out fishing with him at the weekend. Richie reluctantly agreed, although he didn't really like to eat fish.

After a couple of hours of idle chat, sitting in the sun with the waves lapping gently at the hull, Richie was suddenly inspired to declare, 'Phil, I've just realised that fishing isn't really about catching fish, is it?'

'No,' came the languid reply.

Ten tips for bringing your leisure time into balance

When you tend towards pleasure:

1. Write a quick list of *productive* things to do each day. Ensure that you do them.
2. Always do something useful or constructive, however small, *before* you relax.
3. Check that you have achieved something of significance each day. Look to feel satisfied rather than pleased after taking time off.
4. Notice and celebrate achievement in both yourself and those around you. Use the perspective of an achiever when reviewing what your leisure options might be.
5. Check that your leisure activities 'add value' to your life, or 'move you forward' in some way. Always look to have some tangible outcome to show for your leisure time, or have learned something useful.

When you tend towards achievement:

1. Always schedule breaks for relaxation/fun/reflection. Value having 'down time', and vary the pace that you set for yourself during your leisure periods.
2. Set up accessible pleasurable activities (e.g. magazines to read, a CD to play). Not every activity needs to be useful.

3. Make a list of people whose company you enjoy and who make you laugh. Contact them. Build laughter into your life. And remember birthdays!

4. Take regular 'five senses checks' during an activity. Notice sights, sounds, smells, tastes and touch. Appreciate the moment and enjoy the experience.

5. Use the covert language/thinking style of a more pleasure-oriented person, and consider what you would 'like' to do in your free time rather than what you 'ought' to be doing.

Key points to take from this chapter

• We have looked at how the preference for pleasure or achievement plays out in our free time. We have reviewed the issue across the areas of physical, social and creative leisure activities. We can see that our preference plays out more clearly in our leisure activities than in any other area of our life.

• The hallmarks of an achievement preference include a focus on physical skills and fitness, useful social networks, and high standards of creative activity.

• In contrast, the hallmarks of a pleasure preference are centred on gentler, enjoyable exercise, more relaxed and engaging social networks, and passive creativity.

• Both preferences have their strengths. A fulfilling life requires us to enjoy a wide range of leisure interests that both please *and* satisfy us. Our discretionary time is valuable to us.

• We need to make sure that we get plenty of things done in our free time, but we also need to ensure that we make time to enjoy a wide range of pleasurable experiences that make us feel good.

Chapter Eight
APPLYING THE PRINCIPLE
AT WORK

Our working environment is usually a sea of goals, tasks and objectives. It is the ultimate stage for an achievement orientation to play out on. We go to work to get things done. There is an objective purpose to almost everything that we do and productive outcomes are paramount. Work activity is almost defined with reference to achievement. It necessarily requires us to be purposeful.

However, there is a broader acknowledgement that we need to counter an achievement-oriented work ethic with a degree of enjoyment. For some, work is enjoyable but lacks a sense of satisfaction. For others, work is satisfying but there is little enjoyment to be found. Ideally, we are looking for a suitable balance.

Several well-known sayings clearly reference the need to keep a balance in our working life: 'All work and no play makes Jack a dull boy' or 'Work hard, play hard' are both common sayings that reference the need for a lifestyle balance in the world of work.

Work is an area of one's life where the primary objective is to achieve and to feel satisfied. Endless 'fun' at work inevitably results in a lack of fulfilment and a sense of dissatisfaction. Conversely, an overly strong achievement orientation will leave one feeling tired and stressed.

Some work environments still allow for us to drift around and be non-productive. In these organisations, it feels like a perk of the job to be able to cruise. Employees will spend time on the internet or playing practical jokes on each other. Night shifts, being in the back storeroom or being on call are all situations that can conjure up a sense of 'easy money'. But short-term, irresponsible fun is not satisfying in the longer term and, eventually, work becomes a bore.

Conversely, there are more intense organisations with a very high turnover of staff. In these organisations, every minute has to be accounted for and every dollar spent wisely. Employees are usually on performance incentives, where income is tied strictly to outputs, and they can often earn huge incomes. The focus is on success. There is minimal pleasure but the financial rewards will generate strong feelings of satisfaction at the end of the year.

We need to choose our work environments with care and be sure that they suit our personal style. Confucius advised people to 'choose a job you love and you will never have to work a day in your life'. It is not really clear what Confucius meant by love, but if you feel aligned to the organisation's objectives and the demands to achieve are manageable and realistic, then you will likely feel very positive about your work. The money will also help.

It is also important to keep an eye on the reasons that you are at work. It is not necessarily to make friends and be liked by colleagues and customers. You are there to provide a service, and to satisfy your boss and your customers.

I recently coached Bill, the manager of a call centre who had overheard his staff being overly apologetic on the phone, trying to please dissatisfied customers. He had said to them, 'For goodness' sake, we're not trying to get our customers to like us! We don't need to have happy customers; all we want is satisfied customers. Just validate their concerns and invite them to find an agreeable solution to their complaints. Don't bother telling them that you're nice. They don't care!'

I couldn't believe it! He'd just articulated the Pleasure/Achievement Principle to perfection. So often, customer service staff think that their goal is to be *liked* by their customers. Actually, the real goal for them should be customer *satisfaction*.

A number of key lifestyle issues can arise for us in a work environment. Problems might easily arise if we fail to maintain a balanced approach. The following section will consider a range of common workplace issues that arise from the pleasure/achievement perspective. We shall consider:

a) workplace stress

b) poor motivation

c) procrastination

d) burnout.

Workplace stress

Usually, the single most important issue to consider at work is learning how to manage stress. Stress can be defined as 'a situation where an individual's capacity to respond is exceeded by the demands made on them'. Regardless of our abilities, we can all find ourselves working up to the limit of what it's possible for us to cope with. There are only 24 hours in a day, and so our time is a limited resource. Interestingly, there are also only 168 hours in a week … and we sleep for over 50 of them! We often behave as if we can expand our availability to meet the demands made on us. But we can't. Our time and our energy are fixed resources.

The inherent enthusiasm of an *achievement-oriented* person means that they often put up their hands as the 'go to' person. They are keen to make things happen and to effect change. They often take on too much. They are the willing horses who do more than their fair share. They thrive on hard work, but they must learn to cut their suit according to the cloth available.

In contrast, a *pleasure-oriented* person will show a natural tendency to hold back, but in their own way they can become stressed at the ever-changing nature of their work environment. They will be aware of the implicit requirement to get involved. While their approach may initially seem lazy or lacking in initiative, their resistance is basically driven by a comfort with the familiar. There is a natural passivity to the lifestyle of a pleasure seeker, and they do not easily embrace change.

While those with a pleasure orientation might tolerate inefficiencies with wry amusement, achievers can't help themselves from stepping in and sorting it all out. *But we all have our limits.*

Indeed, the most stressed individuals seen in clinical practice tend to be those who are the most capable. They can multi-task, they can operate at many levels, and they can work incredibly long hours. However, at some stage, everyone reaches their limit and stress kicks in with a vengeance. These people have a high tolerance for stress, but have worked themselves right up to the ceiling and have left themselves no room to move.

One final trap to consider at work, especially for the pleasure-seekers, is to beware the excitement and novelty of new possibilities. The enjoyment of opening up new projects may come at the expense of feelings of satisfaction from focusing on completion. Pleasure seekers can often find that they have been left with too many options on their plate!

Two very practical skills can help us to manage stress: *setting limits* and *delegating*. They are like brother and sister. By setting limits and saying 'no', we assertively decline to take responsibility for a task. We can then use delegation skills to deftly re-allocate or re-direct that responsibility. These two companion skills are detailed below.

Setting limits at work

We all need to set limits and to learn to say 'no'. The first skill to learn is to 'empathically decline' a request. The standard structure is to acknowledge that you have been asked to do something but then assertively uphold your right to decline. This is usually based on a stock phrase that explains to everyone that you are 'being really careful about your workload right now'.

Imagine that you are in a bar and are refusing the offer of a drink. All manner of pressure may be applied, but if you stick to your basic line ('Thanks, but I'm being really careful around alcohol right now'), they will give up. If you try to explain why you are being careful, they will attack with renewed vigour. You will become drawn into a debate about whether your rule is necessary.

The same advice applies when dealing with salespeople. Don't explain yourself to them, but simply broadcast your position ('No thanks, I'm just looking'). Never amplify your reasons or feel obliged to make small talk.

When we apply this skill to work demands, the key line to say is, 'I appreciate that this needs to be done, but I'd ask you to appreciate that I'm being really careful about my workload right now. I really can't be drawn on this.'

Initially this response will cut across all your natural desires to help, but the key message is that your time and energy are both finite resources and they need to be used wisely. If you take on something new, you'll need to drop something off your job sheet. It's obvious.

The broken record technique

Walk into a clothes shop where you have no intention of buying anything. When the assistant comes over and asks if they can help, just say, 'No thank you, I'm just looking.' If they ask further questions, such as, 'Are you looking for anything in particular?' just repeat exactly the same phrase: 'No thank you, I'm just looking.'

Say it as many times as you need to before they go away. Do not deviate from the one-line script under any circumstances. You should sound like an old vinyl record jumping on a scratch. You must stick with your own agenda, which of course, is to set a clear boundary around yourself and to say 'no'.

Notice the increased sense of power that you feel over the interaction. You are quietly but firmly setting limits. You are exercising control.

Delegating at work

When a request is made of you, it is important not to simply comply without pausing for a moment. Are you the best person to do it? Does it inconvenience you excessively? Does it align with your overall plans for the day? The key skill is to delegate and not allow problems to be dumped on you.

Here, we learn *not* to give advice or 'fire fight' the urgent problems that are brought to us by others. We never say, 'Leave it with me', 'I'll see what I can do' or 'I'll give Ted a ring'. All of these phrases slip so easily off the tongue, but they all create more tasks for our own 'to do' list. The person bringing the problem can then essentially leave it with us and wait for us to solve it. Instead, we must learn to be 'Socratic'.

Socrates was famous primarily for his ability to ask good questions. People would travel a long way to see him with their problems. However, he would not give advice. He would simply ask good questions that provoked the bearer of the problem to consider a solution. Socrates asked questions that helped lead people to find the answers to their own problems. This questioning technique encourages critical thinking in the other person, generates lasting insights, and keeps the burden of responsibility for change with them. In effect, Socrates held up a mirror. He helped others to see their own way forward. He empowered them to learn to think for themselves and to solve their own problems.

When colleagues, direct reports or even managers come to us with a problem or a task and want us to help them, then we must empathically hold up the 'metaphorical mirror'. We can quietly seek clarification of what is required, ask about competing priorities and elicit potential solutions. We should not be shy in pointing out our own unavailability to take on the request. It will not be up for negotiation.

We are not being unhelpful. We are just looking after ourselves and making sure that we do not become the 'willing horse' that carries more than its fair share of the burden.

When delegating effectively, we either reflect the task back to its source or fan out the responsibility to other more appropriate options elsewhere.

Poor motivation

Are you excited and energised by your working environment? Do you excite and energise those around you? Often, when work seems to lack meaning or purpose, we lose our sense of drive or engagement with the organisation. This is especially the case when we are not involved in the planning of our tasks and then find ourselves just doing what we are told to do. It's very easy to fall into a rut and become bored, disillusioned and lacking in drive.

In these situations, it is important to maintain a positive approach and to recognise that we have the opportunity to establish self-discipline, personal pride and satisfaction in performing well. We need to become self-directed in our work and learn to set personal goals in the absence of meaningful organisational objectives. We should keep records of hours spent on a task and schedule rewards when self-defined objectives have been met.

Often, our jobs are just routine or may involve simple maintenance tasks. There is nothing to show for our efforts at the end of the day. We've made nothing tangible; we've simply managed to keep things in shape. Again, in this situation, we need to set goals that inspire us to keep going, and then build in rewards for achieving them.

Enthusiasm is just a state of mind. Workplaces that facilitate motivated staff are usually characterised by their willingness to *celebrate success.* In the outcome-focused world of work, it can be hard to find time to stop and take time to appreciate success. There is always another mountain to climb, another task to complete or another project to bring home. Often, we find ourselves working to avoid failure or criticism. Work does not necessarily provide us with opportunities to reflect on our achievements and celebrate success.

A strong achievement orientation often comes at the expense of reflection. We drive forwards, always looking ahead to the next target, and worry that by pausing to savour the moment, something will be lost. But celebrating success is an important aspect of motivating ourselves and our colleagues. We need those moments of pleasure, both at the end of a period of work and to mark the steps along the way. The nods and smiles, the high fives, the acknowledgments of progress … all are important markers that help us to enjoy the ride.

Procrastination

Sometimes, we can find ourselves actively or passively avoiding progress towards a goal at work. This can be for a number of reasons. Firstly, we may be stressed to the point where nothing that we do will bring relief from the demands. Secondly, we may have a large, indigestible chunk of work ahead of us, and we can't seem to gain traction or find a way to start. Thirdly, we might feel totally misaligned with the values or purpose of the task, such that we have no inherent appetite or motivation to engage with it.

In all of the above cases, we find ourselves procrastinating. We become easily distracted and may be drawn towards pleasurable but ultimately dissatisfying activities. We surf the net or we play computer games. We attend to junk mail and our inboxes fill up with dodgy jokes and cartoons. Morning and afternoon teas stretch out as long as we can make them, and we become more involved in gossip and the idle chatter of the day. We are amusing ourselves, but at the expense of getting on with the job.

This is a very slippery slope, where a lack of focus on clear goals can quickly lead to frustration, boredom and depression.

The antidote is simple. Ring fence your indulgences and set aside specific times for social networking and legitimate times for micro-breaks. Ensure that for every twenty-minute unit of time, you have an output to record. Make lists of what you plan to do, and then do them! Notice that you've written 200 words or deleted eight emails, or returned five phone calls. Celebrate with a stretch and a quick break, and then create a new list for the next twenty minutes.

If your job involves manual exertion, then count progress towards the eventual goal. Digging a ditch, building a wall or packing fruit are all measurable activities, and you can feel satisfied as progress is made towards a target. Perseverance and application to the job in hand are qualities that will help you enormously, and can easily be built into your attitude to work.

Burnout

Burnout is a term that is commonly used to describe the endpoint of a prolonged period of stress. Driving relentlessly towards a goal is not sustainable for any of us in the long term. Eventually we will burn out. The increasingly frenzied level of activity is suddenly replaced by an overwhelming sense of helplessness. Essentially, we have given up.

We then shift dramatically from an intense goal-oriented pattern to a flat, empty space, where there is little or no pleasure or satisfaction in any aspect of our lives. We lose all momentum and we need to slowly take stock and re-evaluate our plans.

Burnout is not necessarily an unhealthy space to be in. It is a natural physical response to prolonged stress, and is simply our body taking time out to recharge. We feel exhausted, we lack motivation and we can see only problems around us. Everything seems to require too much effort. Essentially, we have reached a point where we have stopped trying to respond to the impossible demands of the world around us and have closed down.

We can often see burnout developing in our colleagues but rarely bother to monitor ourselves for the same symptoms. As we become increasingly stressed, we tend to minimise or deny the effects, saying, 'It doesn't matter' or that 'We don't care'. In fact, it does matter and we should care.

If we can see that our stress levels are rising then we can actively plan to manage them, such that burnout doesn't arise. As we saw in the previous chapter on leisure, it is not possible to charge along with 100 per cent energy for 100 per cent of the time.

Regular 'islands of pleasurable time' while at work are the obvious antidote to burnout. We may have less control over our stress levels at work, but we still need to pace ourselves and to balance our efforts with time to unwind. And, as in all aspects of our lives, it is important that our behavioural patterns in the workplace are sustainable.

Most psychological issues in the workplace can be usefully viewed as resulting from an imbalance. The imbalance may be driven by a number of factors, but overall, pursuing achievable goals while enjoying the ride will invariably lead us to a more fulfilling workplace.

The culture of workplace organisations

Culture is an extremely important aspect of any work environment. It is the glue that binds us together and defines who we are as a team. Culture requires an implicit buy-in from workmates to an agreed set of values, and also a commitment from them to adopt the organisation's purpose and vision. There is also an implicit code of both conduct and dress that reflects these values.

It is important to ensure that, at work, the dynamic of the group is healthy. There needs to be:

a) a strong emphasis on achieving collective goals, and

b) a strong sense of collective goodwill that binds the group together.

An organisational culture can be defined with respect to these two factors.

Goffee and Jones (1998) drew up a now well-known matrix that described four different types of organisational culture based on two simple factors.

Their first factor was described as the *sociability* factor. They noted that a culture is either high or low on a sociability scale.

High sociability is a characteristic of most start-up companies or family businesses. Everyone knows everyone else and everyone is friendly. Play and work are interchangeable and everyone tends to think the same way. Work is fun.

Low sociability occurs when everyone is focused on their own individual tasks and there is little point or motivation to interact with work colleagues. This might happen in telephone call centres, with sales teams that work on an individual commission basis, or within a group of professional consultants.

The second factor that determines a culture is the *solidarity* factor. Again, a culture can be either high or low on this factor. Solidarity occurs when teams are brought together for a specific purpose. The members are aligned in pursuit of a common goal. Their relationships are based purely on their functional skills and abilities rather than whether they like one another or not.

High solidarity occurs in representative sports teams or between subcontractors working on building projects. They are all working towards the same outcome but have been drawn together simply to achieve a goal rather than because they are good company for each other.

Low solidarity may occur when different work groups pursue different objectives within the same organisation, such as at an IT research and development company. People developing different software programs will have little sense of shared purpose, even though they are part of the same business and may socialise regularly with each other.

The Culture Matrix

S O C I A B I L I T Y	High	NETWORKED	COMMUNAL
	Low	FRAGMENTED	MERCENARY
		Low	High
		SOLIDARITY	

Source: Goffee and Jones (1998)

When both sociability and solidarity are high, Goffee and Jones described a *communal* culture, where we feel both *connected* to our colleagues and also *aligned* with them in a common sense of purpose.

When sociability remains high but solidarity is low, then Goffee and Jones describe *a networked* culture. This can occur when branch offices or new franchises are established. We all subscribe to the same values and we enjoy our conferences and golf tournaments together, but we don't have the same collective financial goal. We have fun together but we work apart.

Thirdly, if solidarity remains high but the degree of sociability is low, such as when a lobby group forms to promote a new initiative, then the culture is described as *mercenary*. Here, team members are united towards a common goal but don't need to feel a sense of friendship or closeness. They are there to do a job.

Finally, if both sociability and solidarity are low, then the culture is described as *fragmented*. An example might be in an academic department or a law firm, where everyone focuses on their own professional networks outside of the department and has little need to put energy into the organisation itself. Everyone's agenda is different and individuals may have stronger connections with clients or research colleagues overseas than with the colleague next door. There is no sense of alignment with colleagues or of social connection with them. We are all working for our own advancement.

It is important to note that none of these four cultural types is better or worse than any other. Some work best in some situations and others come into play in other situations.

We can always benefit from considering what cultural dynamic is dominant in our organisational group. If we don't, it can be extremely frustrating for us. For example, we might try to encourage socialisation in a fragmented team that doesn't want or need to feel connected. Or we might try to pull together a project team when there is a low sense of communal purpose or solidarity. Very different interpersonal skills are required to survive in each of these cultures, and very different leadership skills are required.

The terms 'sociability' and 'solidarity' are, of course, almost synonymous with 'pleasure' and 'achievement'. The Goffee and Jones' model shows how a varying mix of both the pleasure of connectedness and the satisfaction of achievement can occur in the work environment. Their matrix parallels the Pleasure/Achievement Lifestyle Matrix introduced in Chapter Three.

The workplace culture will be a strong influence on how our happiness at work is defined. Our workplace is primarily either a fun place to be or a rewarding place to be. Perhaps it is both. Or perhaps changes need to be made.

Leadership at work

Leadership is a highly overused term these days but it is nonetheless an important feature of how we interact with others. Essentially, leadership refers to the *inspirational effect* that we have on other people. A great leader is valuable not only for what they can contribute themselves but also for what extra effort they can draw out of those around them. Their key skill is to be able to influence and inspire others. But how is this done? And what are the key features of a great leader?

Firstly, leaders must have a *clear vision* of where they are going. They must articulate it clearly and explain the rationale. In effect, they need to set goals for their team. An achievement focus is paramount.

Having done this, they are then required to get *buy-in* to their vision. This function requires more of a qualitative sense of 'personal connection' with the leader. This closeness arises more from a pleasure orientation, where time is taken to enjoy shared aspects of the work or life in general. Taking the time to connect is a critical attribute of good leadership.

Buy-in only really occurs when leaders have taken the time to be with their team. A sense of engagement then flows on from this. We need to feel connected with our leaders in order to move along with them. That sense of connection should occur in the absence of pressure or a predetermined agenda. Remember that it is hard to connect with someone when they are travelling fast.

Taking the time to be with one's team, listening to their ideas and making space for their contributions are all essential ingredients for engagement as a leader. If leaders don't spend time in the social club or don't disclose a little about themselves to staff, then there is little opportunity to connect.

'You don't *win* people's hearts …
you *connect* with their hearts'

Peter came to see me as the leader of a sales and marketing team from a top manufacturing company. He was passionate about the business, but was disappointed in his staff's lack of enthusiasm and 'buy-in' to the organisation's goals. Despite offering salary incentives, performance bonuses and rewards for successfully meeting sales targets, he felt that they were only there for themselves. He had somehow failed to engage his team in his vision of how far the business could grow and to see their own part in the plan.

Peter felt that his staff never went the extra mile. They only performed to a standard that worked for them, and they seemed mercenary, rather than loyal.

We went on to consider the concept of *loyalty* in more detail. We noted that often people have very logical relationships in business, either as customers or as employees. They look for the cheapest price or the best salaries. But customer loyalty, or staff loyalty, is what motivates people to continue to buy from you, or work for you, even though the conditions might be better elsewhere. It's not logical to buy from you, or to work for you, but people still do.

Customer loyalty and staff loyalty only arise when people *connect* with an organisation. When people let their hearts rule their heads. Unless you can inspire your staff, the relationship stays purely functional and logical. A loyal workforce, however, feels like family. The commitment is based on a sense of togetherness, rather than a sense of usefulness or personal gain. Simply put, we just like to connect with the person whom we work for or the person from whom we buy.

Peter thought long and hard about this insight, and went away a better leader as a result. The incentives didn't seem to matter so much. Who he was as a person suddenly seemed a more important factor and provided the platform for staff 'buy-in' that he was looking for.

The leader's personal vision needs to become 'the team's vision', which everyone commits to and feels a sense of engagement with. It needs to have a 'heart to heart' quality about it; in other words, a pleasure focus. It becomes 'a pleasure to serve' under a leader who shows these qualities.

But leadership is also about direction and purpose. There is an implicit sense of goal orientation about the role. We 'follow' our leaders. Our leaders win wars, they clinch contracts and they decide strategy. Leaders are usually appointed in order to achieve something. Their function is to make things happen and to represent the aspirations of their team members. There is a natural *achievement* focus to the role.

Finally, leaders are expected to serve as role models for their group. They embody the values and the conduct expected of us all. For leaders, it is important to be trustworthy, to be honest and to be respectful of others. Of equal importance is the need for leaders to demonstrate the balance of fun and purpose that they expect from their staff. They must walk the talk, and they must think carefully about how the organisation needs them to be.

A leader lives life in a glass bowl. People watch their every move. Rather than leave people guessing what they stand for, it is important to radiate a simple *values message* that they can broadcast over and over when they communicate. For example, they could say, 'For me, the bottom line is that I am trusted by both my staff and my customers.' Or they could say, 'For me, life is about getting home at the end of the day knowing that we've made a difference.' The subtle change of emphasis will have a huge effect on the culture.

Seven simple questions about your working life

Question 1
Would you feel more fulfilled if there was more of a sense of purpose to your work, or do you need more opportunities for fun?

Question 2
What is the best skill for you to use when coping with stress: setting limits or delegating?

Question 3
How can you increase your sense of motivation at work? Do you need clearer targets and goals, or do you need more opportunity to celebrate success?

Question 4
On a scale of 1 to 100, how close are you to burnout? What do you need to do to keep your stress levels in check?

Question 5
What is the culture of your work place? Is it high on sociability, solidarity or both?

Question 6
What qualities do you need to develop in order to strengthen your leadership skills at work:
a) a greater 'connectedness' with your colleagues, or
b) a stronger 'visioning' of the goals?

Question 7
What is your simple 'values message' to others regarding your work?

Key points to take from this chapter

- We looked at how the Pleasure/Achievement Principle can be applied to a number of workplace issues.

- A common psychological problem arising from a strong achievement focus is *work stress*. We considered the twin skills of *setting limits* and *delegating* as possible coping strategies, and we then went on to consider how to *motivate* ourselves and become more enthusiastic about our work. We noted that some jobs do not provide natural opportunities for recording and *celebrating success*, and therefore we may have to deliberately factor this in for ourselves.

- If the task in hand is overwhelming, or at variance with your values, then we might well start to *procrastinate* and avoid progress. We distract ourselves with trivial amusements. This can be addressed by setting more manageable and achievable goals and reframing the nature of the task. Work is not necessarily pleasurable but it will usually feel satisfying when completed.

- *Burnout* was another stress-related problem to consider. Unsustainable levels of high pressure will inevitably lead to a collapse. We learned what symptoms to look out for and how a pleasure orientation can keep us in check.

- We also reviewed different *organisational cultures* and saw the importance of providing the right balance between goal-oriented 'solidarity' and more pleasurable 'sociability'.

- Finally, we looked at the concept of *leadership*. We saw how both providing a *vision* and establishing a *personal connection* are key qualities of an effective leader. These qualities are derived from carrying both an achievement and a pleasure orientation.

- Much of our time is spent at work. It is not good enough to simply put up with a lack of enjoyment or satisfaction while we are there. If work does not feel right then adjustments will need to be made. The tools for change are available and we can easily use them to make positive changes towards a more fulfilling working life.

Chapter Nine
APPLYING THE PRINCIPLE TO RELATIONSHIPS

This book is basically concerned with *increased self-awareness and self-management*. It encourages us to use the Pleasure/Achievement Principle to improve the quality of our personal lives.

However, for most of us, the degree of satisfaction and contentment that we feel in life is derived largely from the *quality of the relationships* that we have with those around us. It concerns *social awareness* and *interpersonal style*. This chapter is therefore extremely important, as it looks at our interactions with those to whom we feel close.

Healthy relationships are always affirming and life-enhancing. Whether we are talking about our lovers, our family or our friends, the same basic principles will apply. We look for respect, trust and honesty, and a balance of giving and receiving. If we substitute the word 'partnership' for 'relationship', then we quickly realise what the key characteristics of a healthy arrangement should be. It would be hopeless for us to be in a business partnership where respect, honesty or trust was missing.

In living with others, there is always a need to respect differences in lifestyle. This particularly applies between *achievers* and *pleasure seekers*. Since starting this book, you may already have realised that you are married to a polar opposite or that you are raising a child whose fundamental worldview contrasts markedly with yours!

Two achievers living together can get lost in an excitable world of material or professional advancement. Alternatively, *two pleasure seekers* living together can get lost in a social whirlpool of parties and trips away. But *when one type lives with the other*, then a seriously creative or destructive tension can easily occur!

Achievers will always seem to be huffing and puffing about, straightening the piles of magazines, plumping up cushions or organising lists of jobs for the day. They always seem to have jobs that they need to do before they can relax. They seem restless. They talk of jobs that *should* or *ought* to be done. It's usually easier for achievers to 'do it themselves', and then they grumble about it later.

Conversely, *pleasure seekers* will seem lazy and slow, and are always slightly behind the eight ball when there are things to be done. They'll have a cup of coffee first. They never seem to get off the couch. Pleasure seekers will tend to focus on what they would *like* to do rather than on what *should* be done. They will eventually get around to doing it, but only in their own good time.

It is important that these differences are recognised and respected. They are simply differences. The more driven achievers need to loosen up a little, while the more languid pleasure seekers need to get a little busier.

In this chapter, we will be considering our roles as *life partners*, as *parents* and as *friends*. These are the three most important types of relationships for adults. In each case, we will consider how applying the Pleasure/ Achievement Principle might help us to manage relationships with greater care.

Relating as life partners

Healthy, intimate relationships are usually characterised by three key features. Ideally, happy couples will:

a) share mutually pleasurable experiences

b) communicate effectively, and

c) plan and make decisions together.

We shall briefly consider each of these areas in turn, and we will reference them against the Pleasure/Achievement Principle.

Mutually pleasurable experiences

Sharing mutually pleasurable experiences is the most obvious natural foundation for a healthy relationship. It should be easy for us to relax and enjoy each other's company. We should look forward to opportunities to be together. These pleasurable experiences should occur:

• *on a daily basis*, by developing small routines such as sharing a cup of tea or taking an evening walk together

• *on a weekly basis*, by scheduling regular habits such as meeting up for lunch or going to the movies, and

• *on a monthly basis*, by taking an overnight trip or going out to a special show. We always need something to look forward to.

In addition to the obvious pleasurable activities, it is important for us to note that any activity, however functional, can be seen as an opportunity for fun. Cooking a meal together can be fun. Folding sheets together can be fun, as can washing the car. If you look for fun in life, you will find it!

The importance of just being together

Karen had come to see me with a generalised dissatisfaction about her relationship. She said, 'I want Tony to stop and just "be" with me for a while. He's always busy doing things. We never just sit and enjoy being together.'

When I later met with Tony, he told me that he loved Karen, and that everything that he did, he did for her. He felt that by getting so much done around the house for her, he would make her happy. The more miserable she seemed, the harder he tried.

Like a lot of men, Tony was wrong ... and like a lot of women, Karen just wasn't getting her message through.

Even when the task is a boring, repetitive chore, we can still enjoy our time together. Shared pleasure can occur whether we are busy or not. It doesn't have to be 'all action'. In fact, genuine togetherness usually comes from a sense of just being together, not necessarily doing things together. It is most likely to occur when we have slowed down and are simply sharing the experience of the moment.

Chemistry and 'spark' in a relationship usually come from being playful and spontaneous. Almost paradoxically, we often feel closer to our partners at times when our behaviour seems meaningless or lacking in purpose. Just 'fooling around' can be hugely important. Playing cards, board games or looking through photo albums can all bring couples closer. Pillow fights can be great!

In summary, we can see that a sense of 'closeness' is usually based on sharing *pleasurable* moments.

When couples are swamped by the demands of careers and children, the opportunities for fun and pleasurable times get lost. House renovations can quickly take priority over relaxing, and couples can lose sight of the need to connect. They may need to *deliberately plan* for indulgent times together. Sometimes, we need to create metaphorical 'islands of pleasure' for ourselves when lost in a sea of external demands.

Energising and connecting with our partners should be of the highest priority in our personal lives. We shouldn't have to wait until after the ironing has been done or the accounts have been reconciled before we indulge in a cuddle on the couch. As far as possible, we should always ensure that 'together time' has its place.

A sure sign of togetherness is when couples laugh together, make good eye contact and visibly relax. At these times, they clearly have a good 'connect'. They are not racing forwards towards a goal but are simply being happy together. When couples laugh, it is a sure sign of a relationship in good heart.

If couples do not make time to have fun and relax with each other, then their relationship will increasingly lack emotional tone. We start to feel like flatmates. And if things go on like this for too long, individuals may well feel increasingly tempted to seek their pleasures elsewhere!

Scheduling mutual pleasure in your relationship
List pleasurable activities that you enjoy with your partner:
a) every day
b) every week
c) every month.
Share your lists with each other. Are there even more activities that you can add? Are there any other things that you used to enjoy together, but that you no longer do?

Communicating effectively

The second key characteristic to a healthy relationship is the ability to communicate effectively. Again, good, clear communication is a core component of any relationship between two people.

We often become lazy when communicating with those to whom we are closest. We seem to take our partners for granted. We will make assumptions and *assume* that we know what each other means. For example, we often assume that our partners know that we love them so we don't bother to say it. And we can almost predict each other's opinions on a topic even before they are expressed, so we don't bother to ask.

As relationships bed in, we usually feel more entitled to freely critique each other and to point out each other's flaws. We are also much slower to be overtly appreciative. We become neglectful of the role that affirmations and compliments play in keeping a relationship energised and fresh.

The predominant tone of any communication between partners, however difficult, should be positive. Even if we are saying difficult things, we still need to frame the criticism with a diplomatic expression of positive intent. For example, we might say, 'Please don't get upset, but ...' or 'I hope you don't mind, but ...' We should always preface a criticism with an overarching expression of good intent for the wellbeing of the other.

Criticisms are better expressed as *positive goals for change*. For example, 'You've dragged mud all over the carpet' could become 'Next time, could you please leave your boots at the door.' The negativity of the original criticism becomes a reasonably polite request.

In general, we should ensure that we liberally feed our partners with compliments, affirmations and validations. It boosts and strengthens the connection between us.

Compliments fall into one of three classes:

a) compliments about how we look

b) compliments about what we do

c) compliments about our personal characteristics.

Compliments about how we look are the easiest category! New clothes, new hairstyles and noticeable weight loss all reliably elicit compliments from others. It comes naturally to us to tell people that they look good. The trick is to bother continuing to do this with our loved ones!

When we compliment our partners on how they are, we are viewing them from a pleasure perspective. We are taking the moment to be appreciative. These moments should be special. The comments are pleasing.

Compliments about what we do form the largest group of potential compliments. They are more frequently exchanged between those with an achievement orientation, who notice and value when tasks are completed.

We will routinely compliment the cook after a meal, but we rarely show the same degree of appreciation for other domestic chores. The phrases 'Thanks so much for making the bed' or 'Thanks for emptying the dishwasher' are not so frequently heard. Our partners usually make a stream of valuable contributions to our everyday life, and 'noticing the little things' that they do is a hugely important aspect of living together.

We teach our children to say 'please' and 'thank you'. Asking 'please' comes easily to them. Saying 'thank you' does not. However, saying 'thank you' serves a hugely important function, and we should take every opportunity to affirm our partner's contributions to our shared life. It will make them feel good. The comments are affirming and can make us feel proud.

Personal characteristics are the enduring qualities that we notice in our partners. They are broad descriptors of personality that can be affirmed at any time, regardless of what people may or may not be doing. Again, they are appreciative comments that convey a sense of pleasure in being with our partner.

Relationship counsellors will often ask, 'What three things attracted you to your partner when you first met?' Sometimes it's hard to recall, but slowly we can usually remember. We might identify characteristics such as trustworthiness, openness or generosity in our partners. These are the kind of adjectives that we might use to describe ourselves in job applications when we are asked to list our positive qualities.

Once we have identified these positive characteristics, we can use them as compliments at any time we wish. For example, you could roll over in bed and murmur, 'I was just thinking today about how generous you are with your time and how thoughtful you are towards your mother.' Or, 'I was just driving home thinking how wonderfully reliable you are. I can always rely on you to be there for me.'

Often, we just think these thoughts about our partner but don't bother to say them. However, it is important not to let the opportunity slip by. By expressing a covert thought as an overt compliment, we create an opportunity to affirm and validate our relationship.

An unsolicited compliment is always worth far more than a solicited compliment. Volunteering the opinion that 'That dress looks great' is very affirming. But if the same comment is made in response to the request 'What do you think of this dress?' it will always sound a little hollow. Get in first and validate the things that you like. And always be authentic and genuine in the comments that you make.

Always be genuine in the comments that you make

I recently arranged to meet up with a female friend whom I hadn't seen for over twenty years. On arrival at the café, the following exchange occurred:

'You haven't aged a bit!' I lied.

'And you've aged really well,' came the sharp reply.

Ouch! The authenticity of her comment totally trumped my humble attempt to be superficially nice. But I still felt all pleased and flushed at her kind words — because they were genuine.

Communication should always be straightforward and clear. This facilitates trust and a sense of engagement. If we toss positive bouquets towards others, we tend to receive bouquets in return. If we hurl bricks, then bricks will be returned — often with interest!

Often when we talk about the world, we may feel irritated by the difference in focus when our partner looks out from the opposite side of the Pleasure/Achievement Principle. But it is simply a different perspective.

Our *communication style* needs to take these differences into account. Make sure that you communicate with your partner in the way that *they* would like to be spoken to, rather than in the style that *you* would prefer yourself.

Communication styles

If your partner's preference is for *achievement*, then they would probably like to start planning for a morning by brainstorming a list of things that need to be done.

If your partner's preference is for *pleasure*, then they would probably like to start planning for a morning by considering what they might like to do.

The lists might end up looking very much the same, but the language used in getting there will be very different.

When we communicate, we broadcast and we receive. It can be useful to think of communication styles as different stations across a radio band. We choose different radio stations. Sometimes we want to be entertained. At other times, we look to be informed and guided towards new ideas and opinions. The style of the DJs will be different and the content will be different.

Make sure that the style and the content of your own 'broadcast' in life is appropriate, both to the situation and to the recipient. And realise that you don't always have to use the same wavelength. It will add richness to your life if you tune in to different stations once in a while and celebrate the full spectrum of options across the radio band.

When Mr Pleasure meets Mrs Achievement!

Mr Pleasure had a strong 'pleasure' orientation. One Saturday morning he was lounging on the couch in his dressing gown, reading the weekend magazine. The CD had almost finished and he was wondering what music to listen to next. He thought that he might have another coffee and go to sit outside in the sunshine.

His wife then walked into the room. 'I don't know where to start!' she cried. 'The house needs a damn good clean and the dishwasher still needs emptying. Then I'm torn between working in the garden and catching up with letters to friends. And I still can't decide what meal to prepare for tonight. What plans have you got for today?'

He gazed balefully at her from his indulgent 'pleasure' focus. She seemed pressured and stressed. She glared back at him from her 'achievement' focus. He seemed sluggish and lazy.

The battle lines for the weekend had been drawn!

Planning together

The third aspect to healthy relationships that needs to be considered is the ability to plan together. When we make decisions, solve problems or simply plan for our dreams, it is important that we do it together. If we are bound together by having shared the process, then we are more committed to the plan and also more committed to a future together.

Planning together and sharing decisions is the main strength for *achievement-oriented* couples. They will have a natural tendency to look ahead and set goals for themselves. They will tend to define their relationship in terms of where they are heading and what they hope to achieve together. It is important, however, that they set these goals together and by mutual agreement.

Most arguments in relationships occur after one or other party has quietly considered an issue and then unilaterally announced a plan. This is usually done with the best of intentions but usually seems like a final decision. The individual has brainstormed options, researched options and then decided on the plan. It's a logical conclusion.

This 'conclusion' may not sit comfortably with the other person. They only have two options. They can either passively agree, often remaining sceptical, or else they can object and propose an alternative plan. In this way, an argument quickly starts. Shall we do it my way or your way?

The obvious way to avoid this situation is to start with a shared appreciation of the problem, followed by a shared review of the options available. Couples then brainstorm a range of ideas and suggestions that might resolve the situation. By weighing up the pros and cons of each strategy, they will eventually come to an agreement and a shared commitment as to the chosen way forward.

It will probably be a 'best fit' solution, but if they both 'own the plan' then they will have a sense of 'buy-in' to the decision that they have made. Although it might feel like a compromise, the positive, unifying aspect of adhering to the process usually outweighs any disadvantage that might be perceived by adopting a 'weaker' plan.

This reference to a *shared commitment* is extremely important. Often, we conceptualise commitment in a relationship as a promise that we made to each other many years ago, often in a church. It can hang heavily and feel burdensome. Instead, it is far better to define commitment with respect to a shared vision of the future. This formulation gives energy and motivation to the concept, and provides a far more positive dynamic to the relationship. It is the glue that strongly binds a relationship, and it is firmly based on an achievement orientation. We know where we are going, and we can synchronise our efforts accordingly.

How the balance of pleasure and achievement can change over the years

Initial attraction to a life partner is usually based on a mutually pleasurable experience. We enjoy meeting one another and we have fun together. In general, intimacy only really develops when people slow down and occupy the same psychological and physical space. They need to make time to connect with each other. It's hard to get to know one another when you are travelling at speed.

Invariably, the subsequent courtship also involves a degree of indulgence too. This may include glasses of wine, relaxing lunches, romantic evenings and late nights fooling around. During this phase, the pleasure seekers will discover mutual interests, and the achievers will identify shared aspirations and start to align themselves towards them.

The goal-setting theme will inevitably kick in more strongly for all couples when they move in together or if they become engaged. Suddenly, lists of 'things to do' appear, and savings targets are set. Instead of spending money on movies or dining out, they start to save for the deposit on a house.

The acquisition of possessions also becomes more of a feature and career progression assumes more significance. We become more focused on achieving qualifications, and there is an increasing sense of striving towards goals. These goals are generally based around financial security, social stability and material comfort. And there is often an increasing expectation from all sides that we are planning to have children.

As family life develops, and if children start to appear, the lists get longer and life's decisions are based increasingly on optimal achievement in others. As parents, we subjugate our own pleasures in order to optimise the attainment of goals by our offspring. During these incredibly challenging years, couples often lose sight of each other and become despondent as their own life increasingly lacks quality or depth.

We never seem to go out anymore. We never get to lie in. The opportunities to indulge in pleasure seem few and far between as couples build towards a home and a family of their own. As the pressures increase, there is less and less time to 'just be' and have fun.

During these driven, task-oriented years, we often feel that life is running slightly out of our control. It is only when the mortgage is paid off or the children leave home that we again get the chance to reclaim a sense of choice in how we live our lives. We start to set new, more personally affirming goals for ourselves and to reclaim our previous interests.

On retirement, a tension often develops. Our inherent preferences may draw us in different directions as we consider lifestyle options. One partner with a pleasure focus may want to kick back and relax, and suggest buying a campervan or taking the cruise-ship holiday of a lifetime. They want to simply watch sunsets and relax. Conversely, the other partner may feel that at last they have the opportunity to get stuck in and achieve great things for the community or a worthy cause before they get too old. They want to make a difference. The want to get onto committees or start major projects such as landscaping the garden.

As always, the suggestion is to find a balance. We need to enjoy our retirement years while also pulling together some final satisfying achievements. Balancing pleasure and achievement is probably the single most important consideration to make as we plan to live well in our retirement years.

To love *and* to cherish

Alison, a colleague, once shared a wonderful relationship insight with me. She had realised that traditionally the wedding vows included the phrase 'to love and to cherish'. These days, while everyone talks endlessly about love, we rarely hear about 'cherishing' our partners.

To cherish implies nurturing. I can love the plant in my office, but unless I cherish it (by watering it, feeding it and putting it in sunlight), my love has no use.

There is a pleasure/achievement issue going on here, and clearly, *love alone is not enough*. Relationships also need action!

Everyday tensions

The Pleasure/Achievement Principle often plays out in the daily lives of couples, and unless it is managed carefully, it can introduce a significant degree of tension to the home. How often do we hear of arguments based on who's always doing the washing-up or who's never making the bed? The complainant will be an achiever for sure, but the poor pleasure seeker will usually have been planning to do these things later. For them, it's just that the first priority is to relax after a meal or to make the bed once they have read the paper and had a coffee. For them, ensuring personal comfort will take precedence over getting things done.

Achievers are usually very practical, dynamic partners in a relationship. They bring energy and a sense of purpose to each day. But they do not like to sit still and at times can seem restless and agitated. They cannot sit and look at dirty dishes. They cannot sit on the beach. They always like to be preparing something or checking something, and even if there's nothing to do, they'll start to anticipate what might need doing soon. They are often accused of being unable to relax.

Achievers irritate pleasure seekers, and vice versa. But we all need to take our partner's preferences into account and not get tripped up by the differences.

For pleasure-oriented partners:

a) What are the strengths of your style? How do you relax and enjoy each other's company?

b) What daily tasks could you re-schedule to do together before you allow yourselves to relax?

c) What shared goals could you set for the longer term that would increase your commitment to a future together?

For achievement-oriented partners:

a) What are the strengths of your style? What shared plans do you have that bind you closely together as a couple?

b) What pleasurable activities could you enjoy together and schedule more of before starting on your daily tasks?

c) What interests and pleasures could you build into your longer-term plans?

How to be intimate lovers

In order to feel emotionally close, it is essential that couples take the time to be in the same space. Rushing ahead towards new goals doesn't allow for appreciating the moment *together*. Truly intimate experiences require us to slow down and be together psychologically.

Lovers become lost in a world of their own, where they feel cocooned from outside influence by their love for each other. We 'fall in love'. We 'lose ourselves' in each other's company. We go mushy. Love is clearly not about drive and determination.

Love is not to be confused with sex, of course. The language of sexual intimacy is littered with references to *achievement*. Intercourse is often described as a sequence of steps towards a specific goal. Men 'achieve' erections; women 'achieve' orgasm. 'Foreplay' precedes the main event, and so on. Men in particular can get overly focused on performance and progression towards a specific goal, at the expense of just enjoying being with their partner. They have 'one thing on their mind'.

In reality though, sexual intimacy is much more appropriately described in terms of *pleasure*. When kids are in a playground, they don't play systematically through the equipment towards a predetermined goal. They try a bit of this and a bit of that. They go with the flow and they enjoy both self-discovery and the surprise of unscripted novelty. They delight in just sharing time with each other.

Sex should be the same. It should be spontaneous and fun. There is no formal prescription that says what should or shouldn't happen or in what order things should occur. Couples need to simply lose themselves in the moment and enjoy just being together. It is not a deliberate race towards sexual relief. Instead of focusing intently on the destination, we are much better advised to focus on the sensuality of the journey.

In considering the language of sex, we note that sexual *pleasure* refers to the clearly indulgent nature of erotic stimulation (the 'pleasures of the flesh'), while sexual *satisfaction* is different. Satisfaction refers to the greater sense of closeness that occurs as a result of sex within a committed relationship. We have affirmed the connection between us. This is a hugely important realisation that emerges from a pleasure/achievement analysis.

'Sexual pleasure' and 'sexual satisfaction' sound so similar, but they are very different concepts. They become confused when people are tempted into an illicit affair. Although sex outside a committed relationship may well be pleasurable, basically it will be an indulgence and will never be truly satisfying. There is no sense of purpose or meaning to the coupling, and ultimately it will fuel a loss of self-respect. It represents a self-indulgent breach of personal boundaries, where trust, honesty and openness are the inevitable casualties. We will inevitably feel the lesser for the experience.

In this way, the Pleasure/Achievement Principle makes a grand case for fidelity! For it is only when sexual activity is experienced within a committed relationship that sex can be both pleasurable *and* satisfying. Sex becomes truly fulfilling. It has both purpose and meaning — and it's also fun!

Relating as parents

Parenting can be viewed either as a purposeful chore or as a wonderful pleasure. Interactions with children are invariably driven by a need to advise, warn, control or teach. We are always trying to help them or keep them safe. However, interactions with children can also be seen as great opportunities for fun and vitality! For many, interacting as a parent is a wonderful pleasure, regardless of purpose or need.

As parents, we have a responsibility to help our children learn and develop skills to get ahead in the world, but we also should be teaching them to appreciate the world for what it is. We should be good educators, but we should also be good role models for embracing happiness and enjoyment.

Debbie's perfect parenting moment

'This morning I was walking down the lane, taking the boys to school. As always, it had been hell getting them ready and there had been all the usual dramas. I'd been quite grumpy with them. But now it was warm and sunny and they were happily skipping along with their schoolbags, laughing and playing together. I was following along slightly behind, and as I watched them, I realised that I felt great.

It was a moment of pure joy. I was a parent. I was relaxed, and I knew that this was exactly how I wanted my life to be. It felt like a perfect parenting moment.'

The drive for success and achievement in our children should always be balanced with teaching them how to have fun and to enjoy the experience of just 'being'. Telling kids to 'go for gold' should always be tempered with the phrase 'whatever happens, happens'. Acceptance of and resilience to adversity are great personal qualities to encourage in our children, alongside drive and ambition.

As parents of young children

As we saw in Chapter Four, the main theme of the early childhood years is to grow, to develop and to learn new skills. The education system is hugely achievement focused, and it compounds the natural competitiveness that we carry in those early years. As parents, however, we also need to ensure that we validate our children regardless of their achievements, and let them know that they're valued for *who they are* and not just for what they have done.

A warm, authentic personality is invariably based on an individual's sense of self-worth. This is learned in childhood. Children learn to be comfortable with themselves and with the world around them. They learn to enjoy life for what it is, rather than how it could be. Happy, contented individuals usually feel good to be around.

It is important to model these qualities for our children. Family camping holidays can provide a good example. Most of us can remember as children when we dreaded the stressful starts to family holidays. The tent wouldn't fit in the car, the car would break down and the tent pegs would get left behind. Dad would get angry and Mum would get stressed. And this was meant to be a fun family experience! It was a holiday but everyone was on tenterhooks.

Parents, especially fathers, often get so achievement focused on holiday that they lose sight of the pleasure. But holidays should be fun times whatever happens. If we model a calm, relaxed response to adversity then this can be a wonderful gift to our children. Even if things haven't worked out according to plan, we can still make the best of our time together. In the end, the important thing is that we enjoy being together as a family.

Young children also need to learn the longer-term benefits of *delayed gratification*. When young, they tend to be impulsive and driven by short-term, immediate outcomes to their actions. They will push, shove, shout and cry to get things done. A lolly scramble can be a fearsome thing to behold! They scan their immediate world for the next reward.

But as children grow, they need to learn that hard work is required to achieve more fulfilling goals. The more work that is required, the deeper the sense of satisfaction experienced once the goal has been achieved. As parents, we have a duty to show our children the value of sustained effort, and to help them discover the warm glow of satisfaction that can only be experienced through pushing forward and achieving a valued goal.

As parents of teenagers

As children grow, weird things happen. They move from accepting your wisdom as the source of absolute truth to suddenly deciding that everything can be questioned. Relating to teenagers is one of the biggest challenges that parents can face.

For teenagers, dealing with parents also has its problems. They are in a state of turmoil and personal change. Their natural drive towards autonomy and independence requires them to strike out from prescribed parental rules to achieve self-determination.

Teenagers do not seem to value quality time with their parents anymore. They do not want to be involved in enjoyable family holidays. 'Happy Families' is no longer the name of the game! There is a big world of opportunity out there, and the invitation now is to explore it. They are scanning ahead for different lifestyle options.

Teenagers can frustrate their parents by always seeming to be oppositional. If parents want them to achieve, then they will fail. If parents want them to be happy and content, then they will become grumpy and depressed.

In this way, the Pleasure/Achievement Principle can suddenly flip into its highly dysfunctional counterpart: a life based on misery and failure (see below). Here, teenagers oscillate unpredictably between feelings of deep despair and failure. Why they choose to do this is one of psychology's greatest unsolved mysteries.

The Misery/Failure Principle

It can often seem to parents as if difficult teenagers are applying some kind of perverse 'Misery/Failure Principle' to their lives — usually in response to their parents' desire to promote pleasure and achievement! Instead of basking in lives of happiness and achievement, these teenagers seem hell bent on creating lives of unhappiness and failure.

Despite their parents' best intentions, they will stay resolutely grumpy and unfulfilled, living in a world of abject misery. This is their preference. Parents, and counsellors of course, are invariably seen as stupid, and they can only bite their tongues as they watch their children's stagnant lifestyles fester.

Fortunately for the parents, this simply seems to be just a developmental stage. And it is one that time, if nothing else, will usually heal.

The Pleasure/Achievement Principle brings an interesting perspective to this problem. Teenage negativity can be viewed as either a basic *inability to love life* and themselves (a sense of shame, personal worthlessness, etc.) or else it represents a generalised sense of *failure to achieve* (disappointment, frustration, etc.). Clarifying the theme of the negativity can be an important first step in turning things around.

In desperation, you may well lend them this book. Happily, however, teenagers usually grow out of all this, and normal service is resumed by about the age of 25.

Relating as friends

Friends can easily be differentiated from work colleagues by using the Pleasure/Achievement Principle. Friends are primarily fun, warm and engaging. Colleagues primarily have a functional relationship with us. We achieve satisfying goals with our colleagues, while we enjoy 'just being' with our friends.

Friends need to be affirming, validating and to love us for who we are. They do not require us to be successful, but they will celebrate our successes should the occasion arise. They will also not judge us if we should 'fail'. They will stand alongside us through thick and thin, for better for worse, and they will be there regardless of our usefulness to them.

Greeting friends

On meeting friends with an achievement orientation, they will tend to ask, 'What have you been up to?'

Conversely, on meeting friends with a pleasure orientation, they will tend to ask, 'How are you?'

Indeed, often the best kinds of friends are those who are of least use! The quiet companionship of someone who can empathise or share a moment with us can be an invaluable support. Sharing the ups and downs of life, and even just sharing random experiences together, opens the way to warmth and engagement. In general, the concept of friendship implies emotional connection.

That's not to say that friends cannot achieve or do things together. Friends climb mountains and travel the world together. But when they look back on their shared experiences, friends will invariably remember their shared moments of pleasure rather than their achievements. They will laugh as they fondly remember when they stood and watched the train pull away in Paris with their backpacks on board! Or when they stood on top of the mountain and realised that they'd left the camera behind!

Friends share happy memories. They enjoy each other's company and they offer each other support. The bond is based on a warm emotion. Friendship is essentially a pleasure.

Good friends

'When I catch up with my friends, we just sit around, tell tall stories, and have a laugh. Not a lot gets done, but it's great to just kick back once in a while and relax.' — Nick

---

Men and their friends

It is worth spending a few minutes considering the nature of friendships between men. While women will chat and enjoy just being together, men have a curious reluctance to simply sit and share the same space with each other as friends. It seems that they are only happy when they are *doing* things together, such as fishing, playing sport or fixing something. Male intimacy is generally enhanced by a shared, goal-oriented activity, even if it only involves drinking the pub dry or seeing who can drink the most.

These male relationships are characterised by the pursuit of achieving a common goal. The challenge for men is to learn to occupy the same space without needing to keep busy, and for them to enjoy the simple pleasure of each other's company.

Women and their friends

Women love *talking* with their friends. They bond primarily through sharing personal information, opinions and emotions. They will spend hours looking for points that they have in common. They endlessly affirm each other's points of view and empathise naturally with each other.

A woman will often phone a friend just to see how she is feeling. She will have been aware that it is the child's first day at a new school or the anniversary of a family loss. Men hardly ever think to do this. They seem far less attuned to the emotions of others.

Female friendships do not require shared activity to thrive. Women love to engage through being physically and emotionally close to each other.

Women do things as they talk. Men talk as they do things. It's as simple as that.

When friends visit unexpectedly

It's a Saturday afternoon. You're busy cleaning out the spare room when there's a ring at the doorbell. It's a couple of old friends who've just dropped in to visit. Your plans to tidy up the house are in ruins. You don't want to be rude, but what can you do?

The answer is *to plan* for such an eventuality. We can always keep a list of reasonably pleasurable tasks up our sleeves to share with others. Men in particular relate well to each other over a shared task: 'Hey, let's have a coffee and then would you mind just helping me shift these boxes?'

An achievement focus is often compromised by the intrusion of friends. They come over to enjoy themselves, while we want to get things done. But it's important not to see it as an either/or situation. We can have fun with others while we achieve at the same time. We can create situations where we can run parallel agendas.

Key points to take from this chapter

- We looked at how the Pleasure/Achievement Principle can help us understand our close relationships. We looked at its influence on us as life partners, as parents and as friends.

- We reviewed the three key factors that underpin a healthy relationship with our *life partners*. These were: *mutual pleasure, good communication,* and *shared decision making.* We then considered how the Pleasure/Achievement Principle plays out in each of these areas. We also reviewed how pleasure and achievement orientations can affect the nature of physical intimacy within a relationship.

- As *parents*, we saw how differing skills might be required to address the needs of primary-school-aged children and the needs of teenagers. We noted the importance of balancing the drive to achieve with a more appreciative enjoyment focus.

- Finally, we looked at how our *friendships* can be defined with respect to a pleasure or an achievement orientation, and we briefly considered some gender differences that often occur.

- Overall, it is clearly useful to review our relationships from the pleasure/achievement perspective. Many tensions and misunderstandings can be clarified and resolved, and many lifestyle traps avoided.

- As was suggested at the start of this chapter, the quality of our lives is often determined by the quality of our close relationships. In recognition of this, we need to always ensure that our close relationships provide a healthy balance of both fun and purpose to our lives. The greatest source of happiness in life usually comes from our friends, our families and our lovers.

Chapter Ten
APPLYING THE PRINCIPLE TO CLINICAL PROBLEMS

It is important that this chapter is prefaced with a clear disclaimer. The ideas that are presented here are not underpinned by empirical research. Neither do they provide an adequate foundation by themselves for effective clinical treatment procedures. However, what they do provide is an additional perspective from which clinicians and their clients can consider a variety of psychological conditions. By formulating a clinical problem with reference to the Pleasure/Achievement Principle, a number of very simple but essential truths can often emerge. This can then become a very useful adjunct to more established therapeutic approaches.

The concept of the Pleasure/Achievement Principle first emerged during my clinical work, and it quickly became apparent that a wide range of clinical problems could be usefully considered from this perspective. Clients often responded very positively to the insights that were generated by discussing the model.

In clinical practice, simple observations or suggestions can often provide powerful 'aha!' moments for clients. If a therapist generates these ideas from the pleasure/achievement perspective, then a number of challenging therapy goals will usually emerge. These observations might concern a client's excessively 'indulgent' tendency, or conversely they might show an excessively 'goal-oriented' approach to some aspect of their life.

Significant, enduring, transformational changes can occur as a result of these simple observations. The resulting 'insights' will generate simple rules or catchphrases for clients that can guide their future lifestyle decisions and their patterns of behaviour. A simple truth can cut right through the complexities of life and may provide us with a powerful guiding touchstone.

However, referencing a complex clinical problem to a simple either/or 'dichotomous' view of human behaviour is always fraught with potential problems. There is a danger of making unhelpful generalisations or assuming false stereotypes. When we say that 'men do this, and women do that ...' we are usually ignoring the rich diversity of styles within each camp. Similarly, when we say 'extroverts do this and introverts do that ...' we are generalising to a huge degree. So saying that 'pleasure-oriented individuals do this', or 'achievement-oriented individuals do that' is no different. However, these kinds of statements can often provide us with a useful shorthand description of a broad issue that needs to be addressed at a personal level.

Whether a suggestion seems like a relevant truth or not, it will undoubtedly provide a good starting point for discussion. It will invariably encourage self-reflection. At the very least, it will firm up a client's awareness of the issue, whether or not they agree with the ideas expressed. The discussions provided below are intended at the very least to provide intriguing food for thought for both clinicians and clients as they consider a clinical issue. For other readers, it provides an opportunity to reflect on the application of the Principle to lifestyle problems.

The rest of this chapter reviews several of the more common psychological problems that might present clinically. Some brief comments and suggestions are then offered regarding their formulation from a pleasure/achievement perspective.

Problems primarily related to a pleasure orientation

Self-control issues

Self-control problems are easily conceptualised with reference to the Pleasure/Achievement Principle. It is clear that all self-control problems (e.g. alcohol, drug or gambling addictions) carry a significant degree of excessive 'indulgence' in a type of pleasurable activity. This activity might not be viewed objectively as healthy, but it will always be pleasurable to the individual in the immediate short term.

Effective self-control occurs when the longer-term, more diffuse benefits of self-restraint take precedence over the short-term pleasures of self-indulgence. These longer-term benefits might include financial savings, health benefits, personal reputation and self-esteem. All of these factors may come under threat to varying degrees by lapses in self-control.

There are many different reasons why we drift into excessive indulgence. Some people may be compensating for a lack of pleasure or comfort in other aspects of their lives. For others, a family culture of self-gratification might be the underlying issue.

We usually justify our excesses to ourselves by thinking that we 'deserve' the pleasures. We give ourselves permission to indulge. But as soon as the behaviour has finished, the impulsive, consummatory urge is usually replaced by a sense of remorse, shame and self-loathing. Often, we become trapped in a cycle, where a loss of self-control briefly discharges the tension before there is a renewed build-up of neediness to comfort ourselves. We hate bingeing, but increasingly, we long to do it again.

Binge eating, binge drinking and problem gambling all carry the hallmarks of an impulsive loss of control. We try in vain to exercise control before collapsing back into a sea of perceived helplessness and indulgence.

It is interesting to consider what happens when a self-control program breaks down. For alcohol, in particular, falling 'off the wagon' and starting to drink again usually results from a build-up of small decisions that lead to the 'point of immediate gratification'. We may have agreed to meet *outside* a bar, but it's raining so we go in. Someone is having a birthday there and we are offered a free drink. We reluctantly order a fruit juice, but when we order the same again the order gets confused. A drink is mistakenly placed before us and suddenly the sweet smell of alcohol is once more upon us. It would be a waste to let the opportunity pass. Just this once …

The previous goal of achieving abstinence from alcohol is suddenly swamped by the preference for pleasure, and unless a strong commitment to achievement is held, we immediately revert to our indulgent ways. It happens so easily. A strong adherence to an *achievement* perspective is the major goal of all long-term drug and alcohol follow-up programs. We have to stay focused exclusively on self-control.

The antidote to a self-control issue is invariably based around setting clear goals for personal restraint. We need to establish good boundaries in our lives and to value the achievement of longer-term, more satisfying objectives. Improved health, improved finances and a more positive self-image are all examples of longer-term goals that excessively indulgent pleasure seekers might strive for.

These goals need to be clearly spelt out. They need to be measurable, recorded and rewarded when they are achieved. A highly significant issue that fosters the continuation of indulgent behaviour is that *there is rarely a short-term reward for self-control*. Unless we record and celebrate that an urge has been resisted, then we experience no immediate benefits and remain vulnerable to relapse. The long-term benefits of self-control will always fade into insignificance against the short-term pleasures of indulgence.

Recording and rewarding our moments of self-control as they actually happen is the key to behaviour change.

We need to establish and celebrate milestones. We need to tell people when we have achieved them. We can also do things such as putting the money saved into a 'healthy pleasures' account, perhaps saving towards a special trip.

If we don't insulate ourselves against relapse in this way, then invariably, our tendency towards pleasure will gradually win out again. Self-control is all about valuing and celebrating our ability to prioritise the satisfaction of long-term achievement over the more immediate experience of pleasure.

To drink or not to drink?

Pete came to see me due to increasing concern about his alcohol use. He was 48 years old, clearly intelligent and lived alone in cheap rental accommodation. For years, he had played the guitar in pub bands and took low-paid manual jobs to help support his somewhat indulgent lifestyle.

He would stay out late several nights a week, have many casual 'flings', and his money all went on having a good time. He felt happy and stress free, and was clearly a gifted musician. He had always shunned responsibility, preferring instead to just cruise through life on the back of his musical talent.

However, Pete also drank excessively, and his alcohol use had been getting steadily worse. He told me that recently he had started drinking wine from a bottle by his bed at night. In addition to this, Pete noticed that he was also starting his day by reaching out and taking a 'quick hit' from his bedside bottle. He knew that he was sliding down a slippery slope and that the speed of his descent was increasing rapidly ...

During our first session, we talked about the Pleasure/ Achievement Principle and Pete's tendency towards indulgent pleasure. He immediately grasped the concept and could see how it applied to many aspects of his life. On arrival at his next session, Pete almost seemed to be glowing with pride as he described a 'Eureka' moment of clarity in his life.

Pete had woken up the day after our discussion and had reached out automatically to the right-hand side of his bed for the bottle. He had then paused, considered and instead had rolled over to his left where his workboots lay, smelling strongly of grass clippings and lawn mower oil. Suddenly, he experienced a powerful insight, and his sense of smell somehow fixed the notion strongly for him. The leather workboots to the left smelled 'honest and good', whilst the wine to the right smelled 'sickly and bad'.

In that moment, Pete told me that he 'got it'. He could see the way forward towards a more fulfilling life. A life where he could seek greater satisfaction through a more rewarding job, through saving money, and through playing with more ambitious musicians. From that moment forward, Pete committed to carrying a greater sense of *personal pride* in his life.

For Pete, the challenge was now to live a life where satisfaction became the key driver of his lifestyle decisions, and not just consummatory pleasures. Pete told me that in the future, he needed to 'keep rolling to the left' as often as he could!

All of his subsequent therapy goals flowed on from that simple idea.

Depression

A state of depression is generally characterised by passivity and negative self-talk. A depressed person will tend to minimise the degree to which it is possible for them to help themselves, and they will invariably describe a broad sense of helplessness in their lives. We ruminate negatively on past failure and anticipate further failure in the future. It just feels awful and we can't begin to plan how to move forward again.

When chocolate just isn't enough

Mary had been referred to me by her GP. She had been depressed for months and felt tearful most of the time. She felt bad about who she had become and could see no way forward for herself. She had no motivation or energy to do anything. She felt no happiness in her life. She had been waiting to feel better for ages.

She had been trying to feel better by lying in, eating chocolate and buying lottery tickets. She watched TV endlessly but nothing seemed to cheer her up.

We talked about her unhappiness and the lack of satisfaction in her life. We talked about setting realistic goals that acknowledged that she was starting from rock bottom. We looked for her to feel *satisfied* when she achieved even the smallest of goals, such as watering houseplants, baking scones or cleaning a window.

Instead of waiting to feel better before she did something, Mary learned to do something first in order to feel better. Even though it was an effort, Mary started to feel good.

Treating yourself to *pleasure* such as chocolate only brings very temporary relief from depression. The real pathway out of despair is to find personal *satisfaction* through setting a series of achievable goals.

Clearly, for Mary, chocolate just wasn't enough!

Most depressed individuals tend to self-soothe by seeking more pleasure. They reason that they are sad, so they need to be happy. They will eat chocolate, go shopping or pour themselves a drink to cheer up. However, these strategies will only provide a short blip out of the low mood before plunging the person even further into a depressive state. By treating ourselves to a pleasurable activity as our primary antidote to depression, we usually end up feeling even worse about ourselves.

A far better strategy to lift depression is based on achievement. We need to set small goals for ourselves and aim to feel satisfied at the end of each day. With reference to the Pleasure/Achievement Principle therefore, it becomes clear that *satisfaction is the effective antidote to depression, not pleasure.*

If we can keep this simple idea in mind, then we can slowly plan our way forward.

Traditionally, psychologists see depression as a negative feeling derived from a negative thinking pattern and also from a lack of pleasurable experiences in one's life. Therapy goals are often designed to encourage positive thinking patterns and to re-introduce pleasurable activities. But pleasure in itself is not enough. Taking a walk on the beach isn't effective just because it is enjoyable. It is effective mostly because, on our return, we can feel satisfied that we have achieved our goal. We have exercised and feel energised and refreshed. We have taken a step forward and feel all the better for it.

A lesson from the days of sail

It is interesting to consider the old-fashioned phrase for depression: feeling 'in the doldrums'. This phrase relates to the band of no wind around the equator, where sailing ships would stall as they made their way back up the West African coast to Europe. The loss of momentum and forward progress would lead to a predictable grumpiness and depression among the crew, as they drifted aimlessly waiting for the wind to pick up. Once the first puff of wind filled the sails, everyone's spirits lifted. The increased sense of purpose and direction would reliably improve the mood of the whole crew.

There is a great deal for us to learn from this metaphor in terms of how we effectively manage our mood. Clearly, when we have momentum in our daily life, and a sense of the wind in our sails, then we will feel good. If we are simply flapping about in our lives, then boredom and depression will probably not be far away.

Obesity

Being overweight, especially when uncomplicated by physical problems, is generally a clear example of an excessive indulgence in a pleasurable activity, namely eating. The immediate, self-soothing pleasure of consuming food by far outweighs the longer-term satisfaction that could be derived from exercising more self-control.

The longer-term goals of being fit, active and healthy will all take second place to the more immediate pleasure of a warm, full tummy. We eat because we want to, not because we need to. It feels good. We are driven primarily by a lifestyle focused on comfort, and we attach insufficient value to the virtues of self-control or restraint. As a result, we never experience the satisfaction of having achieved fitness or health-related goals. Indulgent sensual pleasure wins out every time.

Nothing tastes as good as the taste of success

Bindy looked in the mirror one morning after a big night out and noticed her puffy eyes and a 'podgy tummy'. She decided to go for a swim at the local pool rather than going out again the following night. It wasn't that enjoyable, but she persevered. Gradually her goals shifted. She went to the pool more often and swam further each time. She walked briskly for half an hour every day with a friend and ate less, cutting out fatty foods and sugar. Alcohol also slowly lost its appeal.

Bindy's body started to change shape and she felt more confident about herself. She felt pleased. To cut a long story short, she ended up running several half marathons, modelling clothes in a local fashion show, and even appeared boldly and scantily clad in a community fundraising Christmas calendar!

This story is a wonderful example of how shifting from a pleasure focus to an achievement focus can make a dramatic difference. Once you start to develop a goal-setting/achievement orientation, your world can change dramatically.

Unfortunately for most of us, when we notice that podgy tummy, we tend to explain it away to ourselves. We describe ourselves as 'cuddly' or 'chubby' in an endearing way. We tolerate and accept the subtle changes, until eventually we decide to stop looking in the mirror at all. A life of indulgent pleasure thus prevails, and as a result we lose our shape, our health and our pride.

Even fit, young, healthy sports people need to think about balance. Often, they will party hard after the game. They will eat and drink to excess, knowing that they will burn it off in training the next day. But how much more successful could they be if they stuck more consistently to a less indulgent lifestyle?

With energy to burn, young athletes think that they can party and drink as much as they want and still bounce back. As they approach mid-life, however, they will slowly realise that there is no free lunch. Calories consumed all need to be burned. As they slow down towards the end of their careers, even the fittest will start to catch those appalling sidelong glimpses of their tummies in the bathroom mirror.

Highly active people will often develop a weight problem when age or retirement requires an adjustment to their diet. As their achievement focus diminishes, their consumption of pleasure will also need to be reviewed.

Contemporary lifestyles encourage us to over-indulge. We no longer have to actively hunt for a week or two to kill and eat meat. Instead, sugar, fats and stodgy processed food come freely to us in increasingly attractive packages. We are constantly surrounded by more food than we need. We forage through supermarkets that offer an incredible array of tasty options to tempt us. Cheap, sweetened food is the norm.

To manage our diet properly, we are obliged to make careful decisions around food many times a day. Learning to say 'no' to indulgence is obviously the key skill. The balance of body fat and toned muscle that we carry almost inevitably represents the end result of the choices that we have been making. When we see that slight tummy roll, it should be our cue to review our lifestyle mantra. Indulgent pleasure or healthy nutrition? Less chocolate, the universal food of indulgence, and more carrots, the food of ultimate achievement!

There are two broad approaches to a weight-loss program. *Achievement-oriented* folk will tend to exercise more to lose weight. They will go to the gym and concentrate on getting fitter.

Conversely, those with a *pleasure orientation* will try to lose weight by reducing calorie intake. They will inhibit the intake of certain high-calorie foods and avoid snacking. Their program will focus on trying to increase self-control rather than to increase exercise.

The difference between an achievement- and a pleasure-oriented approach to weight loss can be expressed as focusing primarily on:

a) *increasing muscle tone* for achievers, or

b) *reducing fat* for pleasure-oriented folk.

Both aspects are important, but it is important for us all to develop a comprehensive approach that addresses the issues from both sides of the pleasure/achievement scale.

Problems related primarily to an achievement orientation

Stress

Stress invariably occurs when we are trying to achieve something. We have too much to do, too little time and standards that are too high.

When unreasonable targets are set for us, or when it is not possible to achieve the outcomes that are expected of us, then we become stressed. Stress occurs when the demands of a situation exceed our ability to respond to them.

When we feel stressed, life seems to become a sea of excessive demands that we feel driven to meet. Our adrenaline levels rise dramatically, and in chronic situations, we will crash and burn. The physical and psychological symptoms of prolonged stress then take their inevitable toll.

Symptoms of stress include irritability, loss of appetite, distractibility, headaches, restlessness and sleep problems. We may also feel lethargic and depressed.

We are all prone to stress. Even the best organised of us will tend to take on tasks and responsibilities right up to the limit of our ability. And then one extra demand will be piled upon us, taking us over the manageable limit. Stress usually builds up slowly. It accumulates. And unless we regularly monitor the list of demands, we can easily end up taking on too much.

This applies particularly at work, where there is rarely an objective rule to say which roles and responsibilities are rightfully ours. As we saw in

Chapter Eight, we need to develop good boundaries and self-protective strategies to keep ourselves safe. We can use our job descriptions to define those tasks we will accept and those tasks that we can politely but firmly decline.

Achievement-oriented individuals need to take regular breaks to reflect and refresh. They need to learn the value of staying calm in the face of demanding, highly challenging goals, and they need to take time to acknowledge and celebrate success. When faced with a challenge, their thinking style is to energise and motivate themselves. They try to get 'pumped', and the bigger the challenge the more they will pump. They eventually drive themselves to exhaustion.

The antidote to stress is obviously to carry oneself with a sense of measured calm. But stressed individuals will often plough bravely on, using their strength and drive to push on through. They will re-double their efforts if it seems that they are failing in some way. But failure to achieve is not necessarily a personal failure. More often than not, other factors have come into play, usually outside that person's control, and no amount of determined effort can bring success. Unfortunately, this means that the greatest strength of an achiever becomes their greatest weakness. Their forceful determination to achieve success simply compounds the problem. Their focus needs to shift. They need to pause, reflect and refresh.

So much to do, so little time

Clive was a self-employed accountant who was also the chairperson of the board of trustees at his children's school. He played golf and was the president of his golf club. As a favour, he also did the accounts for his local church, and he volunteered for the St John Ambulance service once a fortnight. He also coached his daughter's rowing team two mornings a week before work.

Clive's mother was not well and she now lived with his family. Although his wife did the majority of the care giving, Clive still went over to cut her lawns and keep her house tidy. He had two teenage children, one of whom had recently been in trouble with the police. There was also a recent concern about whether a rental property that he owned was to be compulsorily purchased for a new road scheme.

All of these commitments had evolved slowly and it had been easy for Clive to take them on board. He always liked to help others and he valued his ability to get things done. But Clive was finding it harder and harder to know what issue to address first and he was not sleeping well. He was rushing around only half finishing things and he noticed that it was getting harder for him to concentrate. He was skipping meals and occasionally felt heart palpitations or heartburn when he did eat. He visited his GP and discovered that his blood pressure was high. His GP prescribed medication but also suggested that a referral to a counsellor might be helpful.

It was time for Clive to take stock of his commitments. He was clearly a great guy. He'd taken on a huge range of both family and community responsibilities without hesitation. He was keen to help out where he could. But somewhere along the line, he'd taken on too much, and if he wasn't careful, it was clear that he would 'burn out'.

Clive needed to prioritise and set stronger boundaries around his commitments. Instead of trying to please everyone, he needed to manage himself more carefully. He also needed more time to relax.

Clive, ever the accountant, described his life to me as 'like a bank account where the drawings far exceeded the deposits'. Unless he did something to arrest the gradual decline in his balance, then bankruptcy would surely loom …

Individuals under stress need to review their goals and ensure that they are SMART (specific, measurable, achievable, realistic and timely — *see* Chapter Six). If they are not, then changes are urgently required.

Stress always comes from an excessive focus on getting things done. We are caught between the demands made on us and our ability to deliver. However, by focusing on enjoying the ride, rather than obsessing about the destination, we can find a smarter way to travel through life. And the outcomes, regardless of whether they were intended, are often surprisingly satisfying anyway.

Anxiety

Anxiety is one of the most common problems that present to a clinical psychologist. Some people present with specific fears of spiders, heights, flying or public speaking. But more commonly, individuals carry more generalised concerns and worry about how they are perceived socially, about their security, or perhaps about their general health. We can also worry about wider issues such as unemployment, financial security or global warming.

Anxiety generates an unpleasant degree of physical tension, primarily driven by our anxious thoughts. The anxiety response is a very primitive physical reaction to danger that had strong survival value for us as a species in the past. Physical threats were historically dealt with by fighting or running away. The physiological arousal induced by a shot of adrenaline automatically geared us up to respond effectively. Our hearts pumped blood to the large muscle groups, our breathing accelerated and our senses became heightened. It was all systems go, with our bodies on red alert for action!

However, this powerful physical 'emergency' response has little or no use to us in contemporary society, where most threats are now psychological in origin. These days, we are more likely to feel threatened about looking stupid or saying the wrong thing rather than about whether a *Tyrannosaurus rex* is lurking around the corner. And tensing up to fight is probably not a particularly helpful strategy if you are sitting waiting for a job interview!

Obviously, tensing up physically just isn't a useful response to psychological threats. In fact, the anxiety response often detracts from our ability to think clearly or to plan effectively, when we actually need to stay calm and composed.

Although physiological arousal is the obvious symptom of anxiety, from a psychological perspective it is the underlying thoughts that define the problem. We perceive the world as a threatening or dangerous place. We talk ourselves up into a state of preparedness for action. We become hypervigilant and avoidant, and our thoughts and behaviours feed into the problem. We focus excessively on potentially negative outcomes ('what ifs') and we actively avoid situations that might trigger more distress.

For many years, a key component of therapy for anxiety has been relaxation training. This emphasis on calm, self-affirming and reassuring self-talk to counter anxiety-arousing thoughts remains a central component of most treatment programs. We learn to cope with anxiety by talking ourselves down. (*See* Appendix 2 for a transcript of my own relaxation CD.)

In considering anxiety from the pleasure/achievement perspective, it is clear that we need to let go of our concerns for safety and control. Instead, we need to concentrate more on staying personally calm and relaxed, and to be more accepting of events. 'Whatever happens will happen' becomes the mantra, and focusing on staying calm becomes more important than striving for safety outcomes that are beyond our control.

'I just hate parties!'

Anna was worried about panicking in a public place. She was socially phobic. She worried that people would think she looked awkward and that she would have nothing to say. Whenever an invitation or opportunity to socialise arose, she would avoid it for fear of failure. She told herself that she 'hated' parties. That she couldn't cope. Sadly, her anxious thoughts were now actually precipitating the awkward social style that she feared. She would blush, experience hot flushes and her hands would shake.

For Anna, our discussion initially focused on noticing the times when she felt confident and calm, and from there we developed a theme of physiological self-control. We talked about how she had the ability to control her own emotional state in response to any situation, even difficult ones. She could learn to feel happy anywhere and realise that 'happiness is a state of mind'. Anxious thoughts produced anxious feelings. Calming thoughts produced calmness.

While Anna focused primarily on her ability to feel calm and confident using positive self-talk, she began to set increasingly ambitious goals for herself that challenged her negative expectations. She agreed that she deserved a life of happiness and could make this happen if she built up her self-confidence based on achieving her goals.

Anna eventually found her happiness. Instead of worrying that she couldn't achieve, she learned instead to carry her calmness with her. She reached her goals by focusing on staying calm rather than trying too hard to achieve them.

At last she could smile … she had found the way forward through de-emphasising her goal orientation and embracing acceptance instead.

Paradoxically, the less concerned we are with controlling outcomes, the better we are at managing threatening situations; to stay 'cool, calm and collected' rather than 'tense, determined and stressed'. We can't force ourselves to become relaxed. Instead, we find our peace by simply trusting ourselves, letting go and allowing it to happen.

Of course, the ability to relax is the cornerstone skill for living a pleasure-oriented life. Feeling relaxed and calm is incompatible with feeling anxious. And as the old saying goes: 'Don't worry, be happy!' The trick is to shift from anxious self-doubt to positive self-affirmation in your thinking style.

Obsessive–compulsive disorders

Obsessive–compulsive disorders (OCDs) are characterised by *obsessive thoughts* that drive us to *act compulsively* in pursuit of highly specific outcomes. We are driven by exacting routines and rituals towards extraordinarily high standards of safety, cleanliness or tidiness. The implication is that if we don't do these things, then something bad will happen.

Cleaning, washing, checking and tidying up … with OCD there is an almost insatiable desire to achieve absolute perfection in some aspect of one's life. The repetitive nature of the rituals also clearly indicates that the quest to achieve perfection is hard to meet. Obsessive–compulsive behaviour represents an extreme example of a goal-oriented focus that has become dysfunctional. Often, the goals are defined in such a way that they can never be realistically achieved.

There are many low-key examples in life where we can become excessively focused on orderliness or structure. It's a theme that can easily gather pace in our lives as we collect stamps, file newspaper cuttings or hoard collections of old bottles. The standards become increasingly demanding and we become increasingly driven to 'complete the set'.

It's the same with hygiene. The more you think about germs, the more you will tend to wash your hands and take precautions. And the more that you think about burglars and security, the more you will tend to check that the doors are all locked.

We can easily become bound by 'rules' or routines that are intended to keep us from harm. It feels wrong to violate them. We develop preventative rituals that become entrenched. If we check the doors and windows in each room of the house before we leave, whether or not we have been in them, then if we don't get burgled, we will feel that somehow our routine has been effective. Similarly, by crossing our fingers on take-off, we sense that the plane is less likely to crash. It has always worked in the past! A little superstitious behaviour evolves.

Many people will check more than once whether they have switched everything off before going to bed. For others, polishing, cleaning and vacuuming the house can also easily get out of hand. They need the house to be pristine, hygienic and immaculately tidy.

The underlying concern is that if standards are not met then something terrible will happen. A range of unpleasant consequences may occur. Visitors will disapprove. Mothers may be disappointed. We may fail in some way or we may get hurt or sick. Worse still, we may die. We set our preventative rituals in place accordingly, but often we are seeking to achieve an unrealistic goal.

In such cases, an individual needs to recognise that they are carrying an excessive focus on achievement. They are trying to achieve to an unrealistic standard in their search for reassurance. They should be able to see that there is an alternative perspective, where acceptance of lesser standards would give certain advantages. This perspective acknowledges that a range of lesser outcomes is satisfactory and that shades of grey are okay. They need to accept that the phrase 'good enough' has merit.

In most practical situations, a 100 per cent surety about safety or cleanliness is an unrealistic goal. As an alternative, we could instead value our ability to go with the flow, to accept higher levels of risk and to put a greater premium on being self-assured. We can focus more on how we might respond to future events if they occur, rather than becoming too worried and pressured about trying to prevent them from ever happening.

Slightly lowering standards sounds so wrong to an obsessive person, but in fact, what we are doing is opening up options and embracing whatever unfolds. We become freed up, and usually feel more resilient as a result. The belief that if high standards can actually be achieved, they will guarantee security is flawed. A sense of absolute certainty will continue to be elusive and new doubts will inevitable emerge.

At the end of the day, we simply need to let go of our futile attempts to control outcomes and trust that negative outcomes are highly unlikely to occur. Superstitious rituals may bring us a degree of comfort, but the effort expended is rarely worthwhile. Most obsessive–compulsive rituals can never actually hope to achieve the standards that they aim for. Individuals become tangled up in their quest for perfection, and in the end, it all breaks down to nothing.

Organising your own funeral is not as easy as it seems!

Billy was generally described as obsessive. He sought security in being well structured and was keen to plan for the rest of his life as well as he could. He had made a list, in reverse order from his death, of all the things that he still wanted to do. He was now planning to work steadily forwards in his life until he met his list coming the other way. Then life would become easy. His future at last would become straightforward and all he'd need to do was follow the plan.

The funeral arrangements were all in place. Although he was only 38 years old, over 50 letters announcing the plans for the service had been written and stored away, specifying the venue (his back lawn) and the return address (of his brother) to reply to in order to confirm attendance. The exact date of the event, somewhat annoyingly for Billy, remained yet to be determined …

Things seemed orderly and well thought out. Even the catering had been provisionally arranged. But then Billy's brother moved house. The return address therefore needed to be changed. Several potential attendees moved house too. Then the price of postage went up, requiring all the stamps to be upgraded. Then several friends indicated that they were unlikely to bother coming. They were therefore deleted from the list and other names were added. Seating would be limited.

To cut a long story short, it proved more work for Billy to plan and to get everything right for the rest of his life than it would have been to just go with the flow. The more he planned, the more ill-equipped he became for change.

Billy, like many of us, could have just quietly died and let everyone else sort it all out. It gradually became apparent to him that his obsessive quest for orderliness may not really have been worth the effort. The situation was getting increasingly complex and Billy didn't quite know where to turn.

Therapy soon beckoned and Billy answered the call.

Eating disorders

A key aspect of most eating disorders (anorexia/bulimia) is the strong drive to achieve a certain body weight or shape. The goal that is set by the individual is usually unrealistic and becomes extremely distorted over time. A simple attempt to diet develops a more obsessive quality, where quality of life is severely compromised in pursuit of the goal.

'Nothing tastes as good as skinny feels'

This somewhat controversial comment from top model Kate Moss, in 2009, is intriguing, as it succinctly references the issue that underlies so many eating disorders. Achieving a certain thinness or an excessively low weight goal (becoming 'skinny') feels preferable to indulging in the pleasure of tasty food.

The paramount drive towards achieving a certain body size or shape becomes obsessive and lacks any counterbalance.

There may be a strong sense of satisfaction in achieving an emaciated body shape, but it will never bring a sense of proper fulfilment.

We become totally focused on achieving our goal and deny ourselves any opportunity to enjoy life — enjoyment becomes the enemy. A client with an eating disorder will often become avoidant, deliberately isolating themselves and avoiding pleasurable or friendly connection with others. An extreme drive towards a stated goal always comes at the expense of pleasure.

There is a restless quality to the presentation of most anorexics/bulimics. They are clearly not happy with themselves and are searching for self-improvement. They have strong perceptions of success and failure, and drive themselves towards intensely difficult goals. Happiness always seems to be a step out of reach and their achievement focus is rarely satisfied.

It is far beyond the scope of this book to provide a more detailed analysis of specific eating disorders, but clearly, developing a stronger sense of contentment and establishing a stronger attachment to others would be a good place for therapy to begin.

Anger problems

When our progress towards a desired goal is frustrated, we become angry. Usually, anger is conceptualised as a self-control problem, where the short-term benefits of an emotional release drive the behaviour at the expense of longer-term costs. We can always win a battle by losing our temper, but inevitably we lose the war. We can bully people with our anger into doing what we want, and they may become grudgingly compliant in the short term, but we lose their respect and our wider reputations in the longer term.

We become irritable, controlling despots and people run us down behind our backs. The short-term benefits of getting our way using anger to coerce others are far outweighed by the longer-term, more diffuse costs. We become lonely, unhappy people. Violent outbursts are not clever. Ever.

However, when applying the Pleasure/Achievement Principle to anger problems, it becomes clear that at its heart it is not a self-control issue. Instead, it is an overwhelming drive to achieve personally desired outcomes at the expense of the wishes of others that is the main problem. When we try to force through our opinions, regardless of the wishes of others, then the default position is for us to raise our voices.

Anger achieves nothing

I first met Sean in a Men's Anger Management Group. He was desperately upset that his wife, Julie, had left him, taking their baby daughter with her. He had been physically violent, and felt deeply ashamed. 'I had only been trying to get her to see things my way. It all sounds so stupid now.'

Sean had always been strong-minded, like his father before him. He valued having a sense of direction in his life and knew where he was heading. He worked hard as a labourer, but often lost jobs after disagreements with the boss. He either agreed with people or he didn't. There was no compromise. He had fought his way up to where he was and now he fought to stay there.

Julie was initially attracted to his strength of character. She liked a man who knew where he was going. However, as time passed, he became more controlling. He was reluctant to allow Julie to make her own decisions. She realised that, more and more, an argument had to end in his favour. She would finally agree just 'to keep the peace'.

Sean would use subtle tactics to control Julie, and if they didn't work, then he became physically forceful. His anger was the method of last resort. He would shout and threaten, and one day he eventually hit out.

On reviewing all of this with Sean, it was clear that he liked things to be a certain way, and in general, it had to be his way or no way. Although he tried desperately to stay calm and find compromises with Julie, he was fighting against a lifetime of valuing drive and forceful ambition. In the short term it worked, but in the longer term he always seemed to lose out.

Sean needed to take stock and review his values. To value his *connection* with others rather than his *influence* over others. To decide *with* his family rather than *for* his family. To value *sharing* rather than *winning*. To *empower* others rather than to *degrade* others. To realise that by winning unfairly in the short term, he would never win in the long term.

In a telling moment, Sean told the group that he'd suddenly realised, 'Anger achieves nothing. All it does is lead me away from happiness.'

An excessive focus on using anger to achieve selfish outcomes always becomes problematic. The drive and determination of an angry individual becomes their greatest weakness. It would be hard to use the term 'pleasure' to describe an alternative response style, but being more accepting of differences in opinions, valuing compromise, and valuing an enduring connectedness with others is more aligned to a 'pleasure' focus in life. Valuing the process of resolving difference becomes far more important than achieving the outcome, and relationships with others become more fulfilling as a result.

Sleep problems

Lying awake in bed trying to get to sleep is one of the most commonly experienced problems in life. We can't switch off. We try to force sleep. We toss and turn. The goal of sleep evades us. Earlier, we met Oliver (in Chapter Six), who just didn't have the time to waste waiting to doze off. There was too much information flicking through his mind.

'A ruffled mind makes a restless pillow.' — Charlotte Brontë

Most sleep programs encourage you to prepare properly for bed, slowly moving from an active, 'busy' mode to a slower, passive mode. We are encouraged to download our worries onto a 'to do' list for tomorrow. We might take a soak in the bath or dim the bedroom lights. Our attention is drawn to the warmth of the sheets and the softness of the pillow. We should breathe deeply and slowly and allow waves of heaviness to envelop us. We should invite those sweet old pleasurable dreams to float right on in …

The Pleasure/Achievement Principle tells us that we can't *make* or force ourselves to go to sleep. Instead, we have to relax and allow the environment to wash over us, and allow sleep to come to us. (Similarly, we can't *make* ourselves laugh; we can only relax and be open to the effects of funny ideas.)

Sleeping essentially requires us to passively accept a gradual disengagement with the surrounding world, and is a natural response to the lack of immediate demands. If we can let go and 'just be', then sleep will surely come. Sleep is the ultimate indulgent pleasure!

General clinical applications of the principle

Rehabilitation programs

People usually become involved in rehabilitation programs after an accident or a medical event. Heart surgery and head injury are two examples of this. Any orthopaedic surgery usually requires us to re-learn basic skills such as walking with crutches, bathing and rebuilding muscle tone. Cardiac surgery also requires us to take small considered steps back to health.

The world of clinical rehabilitation is a world full of goals. Physiotherapists, occupational therapists, speech language therapists and clinical psychologists all love to pop in and set goals for their clients. The language of rehabilitation is all about a comprehensive skills-based assessment followed by the determined pursuit of program goals. Although we feel like lying in bed, we are told that we have to get up.

Head injury clients are encouraged to pursue goals related to communication skills, self-help skills, social skills and activities of daily living. They learn to walk again, to speak, to write and to dress. Keeping records is an essential part of the process and lists, prompts, cues and diaries appear all over the house. In short, rehabilitation becomes a temple where achievement-oriented health professionals love to worship.

But the drive to achieve, as we all know by now, should be balanced by a degree of acceptance of what has happened. It is important that an individual continues to live a fulfilling life within the constraints of their reduced circumstances. The constant struggle to regain skills can become an unwelcome additional strain on a person's life. They lose sight of the possibility of being happy.

We should always remember that life is to be enjoyed and cherished, regardless of the setbacks that we meet along the way. The ability to balance a healthy drive towards regaining skills with a good-humoured response along the way is an essential aspect of an effective rehabilitation program. We should still be able to find pleasure in our lives, regardless of what has happened to us.

Frustration, irritability and anger are the signs of a thwarted achiever. Optimal rehabilitation outcomes are usually achieved as a result of pacing oneself, setting realistic goals and maintaining an open-minded response to setbacks and adversity.

Retaining the ability to smile is a sure sign that we are on the right track.

Finding islands of pleasure in a sea of goals

Following a head injury, every little activity can suddenly become a huge challenge. We might struggle to decide on what shirt to wear or to remember how to tie a shoelace. We might need to re-learn how to hold a spoon, and sometimes even to speak.

Surviving a head injury and progressing through the subsequent rehabilitation process is always an inspirational achievement. Everyone is climbing their own version of Mount Everest. Seemingly small steps become hugely significant. It often requires huge strength of character, determination and commitment to achieve even the simplest of personal goals. Progress can be tough.

Throughout my clinical career, I have always admired the dedication of all those affected by head injury, for their determination to stick at it and make the most of their lives. For the clients, their families and the professional helpers and caregivers, there are always more mountains to climb. Patience, tolerance and good humour are invaluable personal qualities to embrace.

I gave my first ever public talk on the Pleasure/Achievement Principle to the Central Otago branch of the Brain Injury Association, and will never forget the wild applause and howls of agreement when I suggested that the goal-oriented obsession of therapists should be balanced with the need to encourage more pleasure in clients' lives. It was the moment when I realised that I was on to a winning idea for a book!

The psychologist's role in a rehabilitation team is often to look at managing a client's mood, which is invariably depressed. There is often huge value for clients and their families in simply sitting down with counsellors and discussing how they can re-discover a sense of pleasure in their life. Sometimes, we just need to put the goals to one side.

It is hugely important to remember how to laugh again and how to experience simple joy. A rehabilitation program is never just about getting better. It's also about *feeling* better.

It is also interesting to consider how a *pre-existing attitude* plays out after an accident and how it affects a client's response to rehabilitation.

If the client was previously geared towards *achievement*, then they will be likely to adopt a highly driven attitude to their recovery. The danger is that they will push themselves too hard, become disillusioned at their progress and then burn out.

On the other hand, a *pleasure-oriented* client will probably adopt a more passive response and will need encouragement to move forward. They will seem to need motivating and may not carry an inherent drive to improve. Instead, they will reflect upon their situation and tend to accommodate the setback with a greater degree of acceptance.

Neither approach is right or wrong. It's just different. The therapy approach can easily be tailored to suit the orientation of the client. Does this person need to be revved up more or do they need to be slowed down? It's a good question for us to ask and one that sets a useful framework for an effective treatment plan.

Grief, trauma and managing change

A common reason that prompts a visit to a psychologist is a sudden change in circumstance. Life may have previously been rolling along nicely in one direction with a stable structure and a predictable future when suddenly things change. An accident, a relationship break-up, redundancy or bereavement can suddenly throw us into a chaotic sea of personal change. We suddenly need to redefine our identities, to establish a new sense of purpose, and to take stock of what really matters to us going forwards.

As the flow of life is disrupted, we find ourselves curiously bereft of direction. Nothing seems worthwhile and life suddenly lacks meaning. We become thoughtful and reflective, and at these times the 'experiential' qualities of life come to the fore.

Although life may lack purpose, we suddenly find that songs have real meaning and that poetry perfectly catches our mood. Connecting with true friends becomes vitally important. Amidst the trauma of enforced change, there is also an increased appreciation of life. We notice the little things and stop to reflect on what is really important to us.

This is a fairly typical process during enforced change. And until we pick up on a new direction and start to think again about the way ahead, we will be taking time to 'just be'. We should never rush through this phase of a transition. It's a real opportunity to take stock of where we are and where we've been. It's a time to remember what life is really all about; Although we might feel 'sad', we can feel 'wistfully sad'. Wistfulness is a great aspect of sadness. We are reflecting thoughtfully, accepting loss unconditionally, and feeling the wiser and stronger for the experience that we have been through.

'To live in the hearts of those left behind is not to die'

This quote from Thomas Campbell's poem *Hallowed Ground* is a moving reminder to all of us of how to live life after experiencing the loss of a loved one.

Arthur, at the age of 57, had been widowed.

'When Jean passed away, it seemed that my world had fallen apart. All of our dreams and schemes suddenly counted for nothing. Everything that we'd planned for, we'd planned to do together. Now, it was all pointless. Life had no meaning or purpose. I'd listen to soppy songs on the radio and cry. I'd walk on the beach for hours with tears streaming down my face, watching the gulls soaring high above me.'

Yet when Arthur looks back now, in his grief he had become more alive to the world around him than he'd ever been. Everything felt powerfully deep and he knew that one day he would be moving forward with a greater sense of wonder and appreciation of life than he'd ever had before.

With time, Arthur was to find a renewed ambition and sense of purpose in his life. He made new connections and friends, and started working for an aid organisation in the Pacific Islands. When I met up with him some years later, he was able to refer back to his transition time as the closing and opening of a new chapter. He now realised that it had been important for him to pause and reflect on his loss before moving forward.

'I'll never forget Jean. She made me the way that I am. And as I moved on in my life, in many ways I felt that everything I did was built on our time together. Jean shaped my actions, my words, and my thoughts. She lives on in my heart. And her memory now drives me forward ...'

Traumatic shock

When the change has been traumatic and involved a life-threatening event, then we might be thrown into a state of traumatic shock. We are effectively 'frozen' in our ability to process what has happened. We remain hypervigilant, we may experience nightmares or flashbacks to the event, and may be easily startled. It may be harder to concentrate and we become preoccupied as we try to make sense of what has happened.

If this continues for over six months, then we may officially be classified as experiencing Post Traumatic Stress Disorder (PTSD). While this problem is way beyond the scope of this book, it is still worth noting that an effective recovery is usually based on acknowledging and normalising the experience and focusing on self-care.

The tide rolls in, the tide rolls out

Josie was employed as a mental health worker for a charitable organisation. She was a skilled, empathic 'people person', who could deal extremely well with her client group. Everyone liked her.

One evening, she opened her front door to find an intoxicated client standing in the half light. He was wild-eyed, wielding a shotgun, and had arrived completely unannounced. He then forced his way into her house and assaulted her.

After the assault, Josie felt shattered. Her life had been thrown upside down. She repeatedly locked and checked all the doors and windows and trusted no one. She jumped at the slightest noise and became very upset at the slightest problem. The incident had thrown Josie totally off balance. She found that she had lost all confidence and could no longer trust in her ability to read people's intentions. She could feel no joy. After six months with little improvement, she was diagnosed with PTSD.

In our initial counselling session, Josie told me that her life felt like 'wreckage strewn all over the beach'. A tsunami had swept through her world. All she wanted now was for 'the tide to gently sweep in and carry all the mess away, leaving the beach washed clean and pure again'.

There was a wonderful sense of natural healing to this image. How often do we see scenes of devastation that seem impossible to repair, only to find that nature has its own way of quietly restoring a natural order.

For Josie, it would take nearly two years before she felt happy again. The primary theme to her recovery was learning to trust again that the world would be safe and that people would be kind. She gradually learned to reconnect with the world around her. By allowing herself time, Josie slowly healed.

Treatment approaches that attempt to confront or 'solve' the problem of traumatic stress initially tend to increase its distressing effect, and such an approach should only be attempted within a structured therapy plan. Current approaches to PTSD suggest that we should minimise exposure to stimuli that may provoke re-traumatisation and, in the first instance, simply make space for our minds to slowly heal. Time should be our friend.

PTSD is a complex problem. Its resolution seems more likely to be found by acceptance and calmness than trying to 'fight it'. If we still feel traumatised after six months, we should seek professional help.

Pain

Pain is one of the most difficult problems that present to a psychologist in clinical practice. Clients have usually passed through a long line of previous specialists who have exhausted a physical cause or cure for the pain. As a result, the pain is therefore deemed 'psychological' (and one step away from a fabrication).

Pain, however, is very real. Although it is subjective and therefore hard to quantify, we all know what intense, severe or chronic pain must feel like. The sensation of pain is the exact opposite of the sensation of pleasure, and this is how we can find ways to address pain, using the Pleasure/ Achievement Principle as a guide.

Noticing pain and discomfort

Sit comfortably in a chair. Now notice the pressure that you feel on your buttocks. Consider how it feels. Is there a degree of discomfort? Do you need to re-adjust your position?

Now notice the weight of your head on your neck. How does that feel? Is there a degree of discomfort there too?

By focusing on a mild sensation, we have generated an increasing discomfort. We have created a small degree of pain simply by noticing a sensation that we weren't aware of before. But nothing has actually changed except our focus.

By not focusing on the unpleasant sensation, and not judging it as pleasure or pain, we can learn to live our lives with far less distress. We learn to accept the pain as nothing more than another sensation in our lives.

Pain simply becomes the 'stone in our shoe' that we learn to accept.

Once we have become aware of pain, we become 'hypervigilant', in that we scan for signs and symptoms. The pain assumes centre stage in our perception of the world, regardless of its actual strength.

Being a purely subjective experience, pain is hard to measure. As a result, it can seem as significant as we allow it to be. And if we struggle to 'overcome' pain, then paradoxically, we increase its significance and the degree to which it dominates our life.

By turning this lack of objectivity into a positive aspect of the problem, we can choose just how debilitating we are going to allow the pain to be. If we imagine pain as a red ball, for example, we can imagine it becoming small, tight and intense, and then relax it out to a diffuse, lighter shade of pink. We can 'play' with the image of pain and determine its 'shape'.

Most importantly, we can dissolve it away and defuse its significance and power.

Feel the pain and do it anyway

Julie lived in chronic, intense pain. Two years previously, she had twisted and seriously damaged her back as she pulled a suitcase from the back seat of her car. Her life suddenly changed forever. Despite several operations and increasingly strong doses of painkillers, there was no relief. She had to sell her craft shop, could no longer tolerate long drives in the car, and could no longer socialise with her friends.

She spent most of her day simply trying to cope. She would lie with her legs stretched up against the wall. She would kneel. She would sit in the spa pool with her back against the strongest jets. Her husband and son would massage her endlessly. Sometimes, she would just sit in the car wash at the garage and let the water stream over the car as she cried. The garage staff would often let her use the car wash for free.

As our counselling progressed, Julie resolved to accept the pain as part of her life. She decided to stop trying to 'feel better', and instead started to set achievable goals for herself despite the pain.

She made dresses for the high school formal dances and painted a mural for the local primary school. She made and sold a variety of small artworks and crafts. She took a real pride in her children's development and she determined to commit to getting the best that she could from her shattered life.

She could feel no pleasure, but Julie was determined that she would at least feel satisfied by the end of each day. Her achievements, despite the endless struggle, were to become an inspiration to those around her.

Without a context, sensations lose their meaning or significance. The thrilling excitement of a fairground ride is almost indistinguishable physiologically from the goose bumps of physical fear. Only the context allows us to discriminate between them and to attach an emotional label. The screams of excitement are fun. A scream of fear is certainly not fun. In the same way, the sensation of pain can also be interpreted in different ways … it's just a physical sensation that we are experiencing.

Being 'mindful' allows us to notice our pain sensations without judging, evaluating or fighting them. They are not perceived as negative or undesirable. Instead, they are just allowed to be. Acceptance of pain, rather than trying to fight pain, is the key technique used in modern psychological approaches.

Instead of a goal-oriented struggle to suppress, which invariably gives the pain increased significance, it is now considered preferable to simply accept the sensations as a feature of our emotional landscape. It is neither pretty nor ugly. It is neither right nor wrong. It is neither painful nor pleasurable. It just is …

Psychosexual problems

Finally, where would we be without a quick reference to sexual problems? It has long been apparent that from a pleasure/achievement perspective, we often confuse sexual pleasure with sexual satisfaction. The phrases are often used interchangeably. This issue was dealt with briefly in Chapter Nine.

There is clearly 'pleasure' in sexual release, but unless the experience also functions to affirm a commitment to a life partner, then there is little satisfaction to be gained. The goal of sex is not just to procreate but also to affirm an intimate bond and connect.

Bearing this in mind, the range of sexual problems can be easily divided into two categories:

a) those where the cheap thrill of physical release fails to satisfy, or

b) those where the excessive drive to perform in a certain way or achieve a particular goal, such as pregnancy, an erection or an orgasm, fails to bring pleasure.

Very frequently, therapists will see couples where the stress of *trying* to achieve simply inhibits the very bodily functions that are required for a satisfying union.

The language of sex tends to encourage us to adopt a goal-oriented perspective. We talk of achieving orgasm or 'completing the act'. It tends to be viewed as a progression of behaviours towards a clear end goal. Most sexual problems occur as a direct result of *trying too hard* to perform. We become anxious to achieve satisfying outcomes for both our partner and ourselves.

Masters and Johnson (1966) described this problem as *performance anxiety* and interestingly prescribed a series of 'pleasuring exercises' to compensate. Here, the pressure was off and couples were instructed to 'just be' with each other, enjoying the time spent together. They were expressly requested not to try and progress to intercourse or to achieve specific goals. They were encouraged instead to focus on pleasure.

Making love or making babies?

When couples struggle to conceive, they become increasingly goal focused. Pregnancy becomes the key goal for their sexual coupling and the pressure to conceive can place an extraordinary strain on the relationship. Sexual behaviour becomes determined by dates of ovulation and clinic protocols. Every month brings hope of success, but instead usually brings disappointment and a terrible sense of failure.

For couples trying to conceive, a pregnancy inevitably becomes the paramount goal in their life. But inevitably, something gets lost along the way. The fun and spontaneity dissipates, and the pleasure of making love is often reduced to a rather tedious chore. Slowly, sex becomes 'just another job' before lights out.

Enter the triumphant counsellor on a white charger, expressing a determined commitment to reintroduce a sense of balance to the couple's private lives!

Of course, fertility problems necessarily require couples to adopt a determined commitment to try to conceive. However, they must also make sure that whatever the outcome, the demands of the process become a *relationship enhancer* rather than an added stress. They should feel that they have been drawn closer together by their joint involvement in the treatment process.

We sometimes have to accept the cards that we have been dealt in our lives. Couples always need to give treatment cycles their best shot and to try as hard as they can to conceive. But if things don't work out, then couples owe it to themselves to find an even greater sense of joy and purpose in other ways.

They can learn to share special moments without judgement

or blame. They can also create a new *purposeful theme* to their future life together. A theme that compensates for being unable to raise a family together and that brings a deeper meaning to their relationship.

Being together as a couple is rather like taking a walk on the beach. You cannot 'fail'. You cannot be 'wrong'. You are simply choosing to be together.

In summary, intimacy is much more usefully considered as two people occupying a close personal space and enjoying being together. This closeness is far easier to establish when the pace of life slows and couples can share sensual pleasure.

Using the Pleasure/Achievement Principle to review our perspectives on physical intimacy can be enormously helpful in finding greater sexual fulfilment. Couples can feel far more engaged if they become more aware of the need to mix pleasure with purposeful function during intimacy. Both aspects are required in good measure, and few would disagree that sex needs to be both pleasurable and satisfying!

Key points to take from this chapter

- We looked at how the Pleasure/Achievement Principle plays out across a range of clinical problems. Problems can be broadly categorised into those derived from an excessive pleasure orientation and those that are derived from an excessive achievement orientation. When clinical problems are considered in this way, standard treatment approaches can be enhanced.

- Different individuals seek out different therapy approaches. As we saw in Chapter Two, there is a diverse range of options to consider. Each has its merits, but some of us are naturally drawn to a goal-oriented approach, while others prefer to focus more on acceptance. Sometimes, a more challenging therapy experience can be created by deliberately choosing our non-preferred approach.

- Either way, the Pleasure/Achievement Principle brings an interesting additional perspective to clinical problems, and for many, it provides a simple but effective guide towards a potential solution.

Chapter Eleven
DEVELOPING YOUR PERSONAL PLAN

So far, this book has taken a general look at how the Pleasure/Achievement Principle can be applied to different aspects of our lives. You may have read all this with passing interest or detached curiosity. However, in this chapter, we now move towards a more specific invitation to make actual changes in your own life.

We shall be considering how the Pleasure/Achievement Principle can guide positive change, and what you can do to experience more enjoyment and deeper satisfaction in your life. We shall be drawing up a plan.

Throughout this book, there have been questions to consider. Following most sections, there has been an invitation to reflect on how the Principle applies to your own situation. You have been asked to review whether your life is in balance or working effectively for you.

There are no right or wrong answers to these questions. Each of us will have a different preference as to how we want to live our lives. The emphasis might fall differently for each of us across the domains of work, home or our social lives. We may choose to seek more pleasure in one area and more achievement in another. We may decide that our overwhelming preference to achieve is our greatest strength. Or we may realise that it is our greatest weakness. Alternatively, we may realise that our love of comfort and pleasure comes at the expense of getting on in our lives. We are reasonably happy, but our lives lack satisfaction. And in more extreme cases, we may have realised that our indulgence in the good life could seriously compromise our health.

By now, you will have a good understanding of the values that shape your life. You will be able to see where you can make changes if you wish. The challenge now is to prioritise these areas and then commit to actual change.

My Self-assessment

In order to get a sense of where you stand on the pleasure/achievement scale, review the following two measures that were scored earlier:

---

1. The Pleasure/Achievement Index (*see* Appendix 1)

My pleasure score was Low/Medium/High (circle one)

My achievement score was Low/Medium/High (circle one)

My lifestyle bias tended towards Achievement or Pleasure (circle one)

My lifestyle engagement factor was Low/Medium/High (circle one)

---

2. The Pleasure/Achievement Lifestyle Matrix (*see* Chapter Three)

My overall lifestyle was best described as Stagnant/Driven/Indulgent or Fulfilling (circle one)

What changes do I need to make for my life to become more fulfilling? Do I need to tighten up and become more goal oriented, or do I need to loosen up and relax more? Do I need to become more aware of time passing, or less aware of time passing?

Whatever you decide, the rest of this chapter invites you to consider a range of changes that you might like to make.

Suggestions to enhance a pleasure orientation

At home

Having read Chapter Nine you may decide that your relationships at home could be enhanced by focusing a little more on shared pleasurable activities. This is often described as 'quality time' with family.

Make sure that you regularly schedule quality time to be with your partner, each and every day. A cup of tea or a glass of wine together? A shared bath or a walk in the evening after dinner? These simple, routine habits can so easily get lost in a busy day. But they are vital to keeping a relationship alive and fresh. Every day, we need to affirm our love for spending time with each other.

Then, once a week, deliberately set aside an evening together to simply relax. Go out to the movies, book a meal out or take a drive to a beach or special viewing spot. Your relationship is the priority. No phone calls, no emails, no unexpected guests. Your partner is the focus of your life and you are fully engaged in the moment.

Finally, plan for 'the big one' every month! Book a night away in another town. Buy tickets to a special show or arrange to catch up with old friends. Make it a special celebration of your relationship, where you spend a little time and money to indulge.

Quality time with children requires us to engage with them in their own world of play. Don't suggest activities to them, just ask what they're up to. Gradually get involved and explore life from their perspective. Take them on at their own level. Look for laughter, fun and smiles. The primary theme is to be together, not to achieve anything or to teach them, but to simply relax and enjoy each other's company. These are the special times with parents that children always remember.

Quality time at home

Complete the following:

Specifically, I could make the following three changes to improve the quality of my relationships at home:

1.

2.

3.

At work

Having read Chapter Eight, you may decide that you could benefit from scheduling a little more time to engage with work colleagues in a more relaxing way. You may need to create opportunities to celebrate success and to feel positively connected to your team.

Fun and humour at work tends to be a great energiser. Gentle teasing, self-deprecating asides and wry observations can help to keep everyone united. If you smile, then they will smile back.

Get a little more involved socially. Stay for drinks on a Friday after work. Go to the social events and use them to connect. Perhaps develop a leisure interest that you can share with colleagues, such as golf or bowls. Find out what they enjoy and ask to join in.

By looking for fun and radiating a pleasurable attitude, you will find that you enjoy the world more. It becomes self-fulfilling. It will show on your face.

Three changes that would make my working life more fun

Complete the following with ideas you can bring to your workplace:

1. A shared fun topic for conversation:

2. A workplace competition:

3. A regular shared pleasurable activity:

Remember Goffee and Jones' Culture Matrix, where the culture of a working group is defined with respect to sociability and solidarity? Take personal responsibility for ensuring that there is a degree of sociability in your team. Trade an appropriate degree of personal information with your colleagues. Make it your personal responsibility to engage with your team. Tell them that you enjoy being with them.

Finally, do not judge events as good or bad — after all, 'There is nothing either good or bad but thinking makes it so,' as Shakespeare's Hamlet says. Do not hang your hat on specific outcomes, but instead enjoy the small dramas that unfold at work and watch the various characters play out their parts. Be accepting as events unfold. Remember to smile. After all, life is too short to be stressed and miserable for such a large part of our waking day!

At play

Having read Chapter Seven, you may decide that your leisure time could be enhanced by adding a little more time for simple enjoyment. You may feel that you could relax and enjoy yourself more in your free time.

Look for situations that make you laugh and smile. Deliberately seek out experiences that have no purpose but to make you feel good. Try waving to passengers on a train! Give a genuine compliment to a stranger. Offer to help out a friend. Do some baking (especially if you've never baked before!) or visit someone who is not well. These small acts of unconditional kindness can make you feel great.

Many leisure activities carry the same sense of 'purposeful drive' as work activities. We have lists of jobs to do or tasks to complete. We still strive for self-improvement rather than take the opportunity to simply enjoy ourselves. We need to spend more time 'goofing around'.

Find moments of stillness where you can allow the restlessness and frustrations of life to subside. Listen to calming music or visit an art gallery. Browse the leisure section in your local library, and deliberately choose a book that makes you smile.

Three practical changes to add more pleasure to my leisure time
Complete the following with ideas for what you can do to enhance the pleasure you derive from your leisure time:

1. A new physical interest:

2. A new hobby:

3. A new social opportunity:

Changing your thinking style towards a pleasure orientation

As explained in Chapter Three, pleasure seekers tend to easily enhance their experience of pleasure by adopting a more 'here and now' approach to their world. They express appreciation of what is around them and they use the present tense. They are positive and they notice the things that they enjoy.

A pleasure orientation invites you to use all your senses to good effect ('Mmmm, that smells good.' 'Oh, that feels good.' 'Yes, that looks great!' 'Wow, that sounds fantastic!') You can give yourself a natural 'cognitive high'! We can all benefit from increasing the degree to which we are sensitive and open to the pleasure available in the world around us!

In addition, try to use pleasurable emotional adjectives such as 'That's a *funny* idea.' Or 'This is a *relaxing* situation.' Radiate pleasure and approval wherever and whenever you can. Swim in a world of compliments and affirming comments. If you do give out a positive vibe, then you often find that it comes back too. Love is a two-way street!

A pleasure orientation towards life invites us all to 'feel the love'! Accept the way that life is, and enjoy it!

Suggestions to enhance an achievement orientation

At home

Having read Chapter Nine, you may decide that your relationships at home could be enhanced by adding a little more purposeful connection with other family members. 'Doing things' together, learning together and planning together are all great features of relationships that have more depth and commitment. You are not simply drifting happily about in the same place, but you have added a sense of purpose to your lives. As a result, relationships become more meaningful.

Purposeful relationships at home

Complete the following:

Specifically, I could incorporate the following shared purposeful activities into my relationship with my family members:

1.

2.

3.

At a personal level, you could also make a list of small but satisfying activities that improve or maintain the quality of your life at home. For example, you could reorganise your wardrobe (and throw at least one thing away!), clean out and tidy the cutlery drawer, polish the kettle to make it shine, knock away a cobweb that you've been looking at for months, or replace a photograph on display with another from your family album.

Try to carry out at least one of these activities every day when you get up in the morning, before your day really begins. And then, every time you stroll past that shining kettle for the rest of the day, you'll feel smug and rather pleased with yourself. As a result, you'll find that you have given yourself regular free hits of satisfaction all day!

At work

Having read Chapter Eight, you may realise that life at work could be more satisfying. You may be there simply for the money, or else because you can cruise and have fun. However, by adding a greater sense of commitment and purpose to your working day, you can feel more energised and fulfilled. We all spend too much time at work for it to simply be a means to an end. Time at work needs to be personally meaningful.

Often, we find that although we are clearly achievement focused at work, we are so busy responding to the demands and targets set by others that we don't set goals for our own advancement or satisfaction.

In order to bring a greater sense of personal achievement to your work, you could consider the following changes.

In the short term, at the start of each day, make a list of things that you want to achieve for yourself. Tick them off as you go. You may want to delete redundant emails from your inbox, set up a meeting for your own career development, return non-urgent phone calls or conclude a work commitment that has been dribbling on for too long. Kill it.

The key theme here is to be pulling things together, closing them down and arriving at an endpoint. Resist the urge to open things up or to create options. Remember to set boundaries and to say 'no'.

As your day progresses, make sure that you are crossing items off your 'to do' list. Turn your 'to do' list into a 'things done' list. And then, at the end of the day, you can look back with satisfaction at all the small things that you have achieved for yourself.

In the long term, our working lives usually unfold in response to circumstance. Opportunities for promotion may arise for us every now and then, and sometimes we get shifted around during restructuring exercises. Sometimes we are sidelined completely. Sometimes the organisation dissolves around us.

We rarely get opportunities in our working lives to routinely review where we are going or to plan our career path with any sense of control. The optimistic plans of our youth give way to a more measured acceptance of the workplace as a constrained environment, where we do the best we can to get ahead.

However, it is important not to fall into passive acceptance. We can identify choices and make decisions and steer a more assertive course through our working lives. It is well worth arranging a trip to see a career planner on a regular basis, to identify key personal drivers/values and to set goals for getting to where you would like to be. Set 'audacious' goals. Dream expansively about what your future might look like and don't be constrained by your current circumstances.

There will always be an opportunity for you to 'take a step up' at work, and you can define this wonderful phrase in any way that you wish. Always be looking to go 'onwards and upwards'!

At play

Having read Chapter Seven, you may realise that your leisure time is based more on fun than satisfaction. You could challenge yourself more and explore opportunities to broaden your experience of life. You could build in more opportunities to learn and develop new skills. It is important not to see your leisure hours as simply 'down time'. Simple relaxation and fun are not enough to feel fulfilled.

In the *garden,* you could start with simple tidying or maintenance tasks. Sweep the entrance to your house or water the plants. Start small and build momentum as you go. Gradually develop your plan for the day, and when you eventually sit down to relax, look around and feel satisfied at the changes you have made.

For *fitness,* establish a regular pattern of walking for a minimum of 10 minutes every day. Schedule three 30-minute exercise sessions for yourself every week, and stick to the arrangements! Jogging, swimming, cycling or hard gardening are all easy activities to build into your life. Keep records of your times. You'll be amazed at how quickly changes start to occur.

Also set a goal to *learn something new* each day. Practise playing a musical instrument, learn a few words in a new language, or study towards a practical qualification. For example, you could enrol in a program to qualify as a junior sports coach. Or you could learn to windsurf. Or perhaps you could take a barista class to learn to make good coffee. There are endless possibilities.

Socially, you could strike up an arrangement with a friend to achieve any of the above goals together. Achieving objectives with friends truly enhances relationships that are otherwise based simply on having fun. You do things together (e.g. quilting, woodwork or perhaps learning conversational French) in addition to just enjoying each other's company.

Three practical changes to add more achievement to your life
Complete the following with practical changes you can make right now in each of the three areas to add more achievement to your life:
1. At home:
2. At work:
3. At play:

Changing your thinking style towards an achievement orientation

An achievement orientation requires us to look optimistically towards the future. In Chapter One, we saw how an achievement orientation focuses on what *needs* to be done. There is an anticipation of satisfaction if hard work is endured. Effort is valued and is seen as the gateway to a fulfilling life.

An achievement orientation looks outwards and towards what needs to be done in the future. It looks at how things could be rather than how things are. Achievers tend to challenge convention and to set goals for change. The self-talk becomes speculative. In the words of George Bernard Shaw, 'Some men see things as they are and ask why. Others dream things that never were and ask why not.'

There are always bigger mountains to climb and larger problems to solve. They notice what's been done, and more importantly they notice what needs to be done. They rarely bother to acknowledge the pleasure of the moment. Their language is usually couched in the future tense.

Achievers tend to energise themselves by using imperatives, such as 'we should' or 'we ought', and they use emotional adjectives such as 'intriguing', 'curious' and 'fascinating' to describe their world. Achievers thrive on challenges, and to them, life is full of invitations to test themselves against the expectations of themselves and others. They wake up eager to see what the day might have to offer them.

They are usually 'morning people'.

Planning for the next phase of your life

People who pick up this type of self-help book are invariably slightly dissatisfied with their lives. They are searching for change. They have a vague sense of dissatisfaction with life as it stands and wonder about the changes that they could make.

As they wait for their flight to be called, they mooch around the self-help books at the airport and they dream. Or as they rush through a bookshop looking for a birthday card, they slow up past the self-help display. They wonder what could be different in their lives, and they casually pick up a book like this …

In Chapter Four we reviewed the seven stages of life and filled out an exercise where we charted the balance of pleasure and achievement in our lives so far. Now, as we look ahead, we can stop and consider whether we want to continue along the path that we have set for ourselves, or whether we wish to deliberately break the mould and explore life through a different lens. There is no right or wrong decision to be made here. It's just a matter of stopping to consider the key values that you want to shape your life going forward.

Should we 'tighten up', set goals and strive towards achieving satisfying changes, or should we 'slacken off', relax and enjoy the place that we are at. There are no rights; there are no wrongs. There are simply big picture lifestyle decisions to be made … if you pause, reflect and deliberately choose to make them.

Sharing your plan

We often make personal plans to change aspects of our lives. We can plan for change as we lie in the bath, as we swim lengths of a pool or as we walk in the park. But the evidence shows that planning for change by oneself rarely leads to sustainable outcomes. The planning never quite seems to reach a definitive point where a firm commitment is made. There are always 'maybes, 'ifs', and 'probablys' involved. Excuses abound. It is all too easy for us to excuse ourselves and to renege on a personal promise. After all, no one will ever know!

Sharing a plan for lifestyle change with another person adds huge value to the commitment. It makes it more likely that changes will occur. This is why support groups, counsellors and therapists are so useful. A promise witnessed by others is a promise that will be under constant scrutiny. The external accountability adds a dimension of objectivity that cannot be so easily dismissed or reasoned away.

In addition, it is useful to *add timelines and review dates* to your proposed changes. Nothing need be set in stone, but you do need to set a clearly defined length of time to experiment with change. An example might be: 'Over the next six months, I am going to go for a coffee with Sandy at the gym before heading back to work.' Or, 'Every Saturday morning until Christmas, I am going to wash the car before breakfast.'

These simple changes need to be declared to someone else, either a family member or a friend. This doesn't need to be a big deal, but you need to simply ask them to check up on how you're going. The conversation could be, 'Hey, I've just been thinking about how I need to tighten up/loosen up in my life. I've decided to ... Would you mind if I kept you updated about how I'm going?'

All lifestyle changes are reinforced by this type of informal contract with a 'significant other'. Someone whom we can trust to keep us aligned with our core values.

Question 1

Who will you use to help encourage the changes identified above?

Question 2

How will you schedule regular interviews with them?

Committing to changes in our lives

There are two naturally occurring opportunities in life for us to commit to making significant changes.

1. New Year's resolutions

Every New Year's Eve, we usually try to make 'resolutions' to change some aspect of our life. Next time you are faced with this daunting task, try to use the Pleasure/Achievement Principle to give added traction to your plan.

You will know by now that your resolutions should be towards either:

a) curbing indulgence and increasing achievement, or

b) slackening off from pushing too hard and letting a little more pleasure back into your life.

Resolve to bring 'balance' to your life and find more richness.

2. Bucket lists

It has recently become increasingly fashionable to write down a 'bucket list' of things that you want to do before you die.

Your bucket list will usually show up your preference for either pleasure or achievement. However, it also gives you a great opportunity to consider the other type of experiences/activities that you have not got around to doing because of your personal preference.

Try jotting down a quick list of things that you have yet to explore. Remember to include experiences from your *less preferred* value system in addition to the easy items that derive from your natural tendency towards achievement or pleasure.

Again, look to create a richness and variety of life experiences that give both breadth and depth to your personal story.

It would be a huge mistake to casually put this book aside before seriously committing to a definitive plan for personal change, however small. Unless you live a life of perfect balance and feel a sense of total fulfilment, then you will need to 'trim your sails' at the very least. (Of course, if you do happen to be living a totally fulfilling life, then you probably won't be reading this book!)

All self-help books allow us to identify key issues in our lives, and they all offer suggestions on how to address them. In this book, the central 'pleasure/achievement issue' is a broad, sweeping theme, but it carries with it some very specific, practical implications. Throughout the chapters, there are implicit invitations for you to make changes to the way that you live your life.

Your personal plan is where the 'rubber hits the road'. We can talk as much as we like about ourselves, but until we make actual changes, it all counts for nothing. So now is the time for us to move from the 'awareness and planning' stage of a project, and shift firmly into the *implementation phase!*

Should we be tightening up or loosening up? Should we be digging deeper or letting go? Should we go harder, or slacken off? By now, you will have some clear ideas about how you might bring a greater sense of fulfilment to various aspects of your own life.

There is little more talking to be done. It is now time for you to make the positive changes that you would like to see in your life. Personally commit to making actual change *now*, and then go out and tell the world!

Important!

Make sure that you actually bother to implement your plan and give yourself the best possible chance to live a complete and fulfilling life!

Chapter Twelve
TOWARDS A LIFE WELL LIVED

When the Irish golfer Padraig Harrington won the British Open Golf Championship for the first time in 2007, he described the feeling as, 'Unbelievable. It was like a bottle of champagne exploding in my head.' He described a euphoric state of pure elation. He described feelings of surprise, joy and total amazement that he had won.

The following year Padraig, against all odds, won again. This time, the weather was shocking, and Padraig had been plagued with a wrist injury that had threatened to force him out of the competition. Despite all this, he somehow dug deep and won again, coming from behind in a tense final round. When asked how the feeling compared with his win the year before, he declared that it was different. This time, he described an overwhelming sense of pride in his achievement. He was almost subdued in his response, but quietly described the win as probably the most immensely satisfying day in his life.

In a nutshell, Padraig was describing the Pleasure/Achievement Principle. The Principle had been played out for him with all of its simplicity and with all of its subtlety. The same event (winning the British Open), when experienced under different circumstances and with different expectations and perspectives, had resulted in two very different emotional states. What a lucky guy he was — he'd found happiness at both ends of the scale!

More recently the veteran golfer Bob Charles, starting in the New Zealand Open at the ripe old age of 72, was asked what goals he had set for himself in the competition. Interestingly, he replied that he was not the kind of guy who set goals, but focused instead on just playing the game that he loved.

Again, the underlying values system is crystal clear.

•

You have probably found that since dipping into *When Happiness is Not Enough*, you have started applying the Pleasure/Achievement Principle to almost everything that you do, say or hear.

Every morning, when the alarm goes off, you will decide whether to get up and start the day or roll over for an extra 10-minute snooze. And when you do get up, the next decision will be whether to first have a cup of coffee and read the paper or put on a load of washing. The day, with all its small decision points, will have started to unfold.

When you watch TV, you will again notice the balance of pleasure and achievement that is available. Programmers will probably seem to over-emphasise the role of entertainment on TV at the expense of education or useful information. The TV news will seem to counterbalance stories that 'inform and educate' us with stories that 'entertain or amuse' us. Magazines will also provide sensible advice for achieving healthy lifestyles through diet and exercise, balanced with tantalising gossip and recipes for mouthwatering indulgent desserts.

But do the media have the balance right? And do *you* have the balance right in terms of what you watch and what you read?

Our lives develop a natural flow, with circumstance playing a large part in drawing us forward or sometimes holding us back. We have lots of opportunities in our daily lives to either get more things done or to take more time out. Different situations and different opportunities can be sought out and used to our advantage.

Waiting for a bus or a train can become an opportunity to be savoured rather than a frustration to avoid. It's potentially a great time for reflection. It's a time to be more appreciative and to be more relaxed. These naturally occurring periods of enforced time out from progress towards a goal allow us to be more 'in the moment'.

Conversely, when we have been enjoying a quiet soak in the bath, the phone ringing can be the perfect cue for us to switch back into 'action mode'. We get out of the bath and we get on with the day. This time, the interruption serves to disengage us from reflection and to re-engage us with getting the most from the day.

'Did we win the ballet?'

At the tender age of seven, sports-mad Henry watched his mum and big sister head out to the ballet for the evening. On their return, he casually inquired, 'Did we win?'

It was a good question. It showed an interest in what his sister was doing. The trouble is, Henry, no one ever wins the ballet! It's basically just a pleasure thing …

By now, you will have a much clearer basis upon which to make a considered response to situations as they arise. You will be more aware of whether it's time for you to kick back and relax, or time for you to become energised for action. Simple decisions, such as being asked if you would like a glass of wine or a cup of coffee, suddenly take on a more incisive edge.

Useful desserts

A while ago, I was sitting in a restaurant with a friend looking at the dessert menu. Having scanned the page, he casually remarked, 'These desserts are all comfort foods. There's nothing refreshing or cleansing on the dessert menu at all!'

Even when the perfect opportunity had presented itself for him to indulge, he had found the need to set a little 'cleansing or refreshing' goal for himself! You'll be pleased to know that after a little persuasion, he allowed himself to indulge in just a little pleasure. He shared my chocolate mud cake with me!

Everyday phrases can also suddenly seem to carry added significance. For example, the saying 'I wouldn't do it for love nor money' makes a clear reference to personal pleasure or personal gain as the only two reasons to do something.

A yacht might be described as someone's 'pride and joy'. This phrase makes clear reference to the 'pride' in the achievements gained and also the 'joy' of the experience when sailing her. Similarly, the phrases 'business or pleasure' and 'work and play' highlight the same fundamental dichotomy in our lives. A shop might advertise 'friendly and efficient service', drawing attention to the need for both pleasurable and purposeful interactions between the staff and their customers.

Bantams for pleasure and profit!

When I was a young boy, one of my favourite books was a battered old paperback produced in Britain during World War II. It gave advice about keeping bantams in the backyard. Not only would bantams produce eggs for next to nothing but they also made great pets.

> I came across the book again recently and the title struck me with renewed power. *Bantams for Pleasure and Profit* — such a great line. No wonder it had such popular appeal!

The business and sporting worlds are also rife with phrases that tend to encourage an achievement perspective. For example, 'Make every post a winning post' is just one example of a sporting phrase that serves to energise and drive us forward. We are continually encouraged to keep our eye on the prize.

Conversely, *music and the arts* tend to encourage more of a pleasure perspective. The invitation is to be open to the experience of sensory pleasure. However, this is not always entirely the case. Most dreamy love songs and tuneful ballads will appeal more to our pleasure instincts, while angry, driving rock themes invariably suggest energy and call us to action. Clearly, it pays to think quite carefully about your choice of music before you push play. The wrong selection could ruin your plans for the rest of the day!

As we gradually pull together our key learnings from *When Happiness is Not Enough*, and reflect on the action plan that was generated in Chapter Eleven, we can clarify our self-awareness and our increased ability to lead a more fulfilling life.

We all have an innate tendency to act in one or other of the two lifestyle orientations. This tendency is then either enhanced or moderated by our culture, our family values and our social context. As a result, we gradually develop a thinking style and a worldview that drives habits and enduring patterns of behaviour. We barely notice the subtle bias that has crept into our lives. People around us all think the same way as us, and they reinforce the values that we hold.

This book opens our eyes to a simple truth that colours the way we live our lives. A fish swims through water but doesn't see it. We breathe oxygen but don't see it. We live in a world of achievement or pleasure, but we don't see it.

For each of us, becoming aware of our preference with regard to lifestyle values gives us a wonderful opportunity for personal development. We can learn to curb the excesses of our dominant preference and to explore the potential of our non-dominant preference. We can learn to live our life in greater balance.

At the end of the day, do we look back and remember the pleasure that we've had, or do we remember the things that we've achieved? And at the end of our lives, will we look back and be happy with the balance that we have struck?

There seems to be a fundamental, innate attraction for us all to seek out the pleasurable experiences that life has to offer. It's an almost primal drive to seek contentment in life; to be well fed, drowsy and warm. It could be said that we all spend our lives searching for this state of perfect bliss. But in addition to this type of happiness, there is another quality to life that we can all admire.

Most of us also carry a generalised curiosity, and search for personal development and greater knowledge. We hope to make a difference to the world around us. In this way, it seems that we also carry a primal drive to leave a legacy, and to know that we have made a difference during our time on the planet.

During every minute of every day, we make small decisions that either move us towards feelings of contentment or towards feelings of satisfaction from getting things done. These seem to be cumulative patterns of behaviour, and enduring themes inevitably develop in our habits and attitudes.

In order to live a happier life, do we personally need to experience more pleasure or more satisfaction? It's an important question, because in order to live a truly fulfilling life, it's clear that we need to experience a healthy balance of both.

Pleasure requires us to engage fully with the world around us using our senses, while achievement requires us to interact robustly with the world using our muscular strength. Intriguingly, both bodily systems connect strongly through the heart. Sensory stimulation brings joy to our heart, while our heart also drives our muscles towards satisfying achievement and success.

Simply 'being happy' is clearly not enough. To live passionately, we need to engage joyfully with the world around us but also strive determinedly to make a difference. At special times, we should be able to feel our hearts soaring with joy as we marvel at the experience of being alive. At other times, we should be able to feel our hearts glowing with pride as we stand on top of our personal mountain.

When we live our lives expansively in this way, we will inevitably find ourselves experiencing a more fulfilling life. It will be a life where we 'work hard' and we 'play hard'. It will be a life where we feel both 'pride' and 'joy'. And it will be a life where we enjoy an abundance of both 'satisfaction' and 'pleasure'. In short, it will be a happy and fulfilling life.

It will be a life well lived.

FREQUENTLY ASKED QUESTIONS

Q: 'I enjoy achieving things; it's all one and the same to me. My work is
        my pleasure. There's really no difference.'

A: That may be true, but beware of confusing the feelings of *pleasure* and
        satisfaction. The words mean different things. This is the key concept
        promoted in *When Happiness is Not Enough*. We need to identify more
        carefully what the *primary driver* for our actions might be.

        We saw earlier that work can almost be defined as behaviour that
        is driven by achievement, regardless of the degree of pleasure
        involved. Primarily, we tend to go to work to achieve satisfactory
        outcomes, not to have fun. But when both factors are aligned, as
        perhaps in your case, then that's a great place to be. And be sure that
        they stay in balance.

Q: 'I work hard and I play hard. Surely it's not the balance between
        pleasure and achievement that is important, but the degree to which
        you push each aspect of your life?'

A: Working hard and playing hard sounds suspiciously like an
        achievement orientation might be playing out in both areas of your
        life. However, we all have varying capacities to live life to the full and

some people have an almost boundless ability to indulge fully in the pleasures of life while also getting loads of things done. Successful entertainers and media stars are often good examples of this. For others, neither pleasure nor achievement comes particularly easily.

While an excessive focus on either indulgence or ambition often leads to one's downfall, an excess of both can be doubly dangerous! To live a fulfilling life does not necessarily mean having your foot down hard on the accelerator all the time. We should always pace ourselves to live within our capacity to sustain our physical and mental wellbeing.

If you push neither aspect in your life, and you have no fun and no drive, then you might as well be dead! It is important to monitor the degree to which we push ourselves towards both pleasure and achievement and to spread our investment of both time and energy as best we can.

I find that the Pleasure/Achievement Lifestyle Matrix described in Chapter Three addresses the issue that you raise quite well. In Appendix 1, we derived a score to describe our degree of *engagement* in life, which is very similar to the idea that you are suggesting. Ideally, I would suggest that it is good to be highly engaged, where both achievement and pleasure are sought out in good measure.

Q: 'Where do you stand personally with regard to the Pleasure/Achievement Principle?'

A: 'I have a clear tendency to drift towards pleasure if I don't actively manage myself. I'll generally end up on the couch, at the beach or at a party! Writing this book was an enormous achievement for me in this regard. Although it's been hugely enjoyable to write, primarily I needed to learn the discipline of achieving certain outcomes every day, and to set myself deadlines to work towards.

I learned to value the feelings of satisfaction that come from having achieved something each day, rather than continuing with my natural tendency to procrastinate and indulge in the easy pleasures of an enjoyable lifestyle.

I kept continuous records of how many hours I spent writing each week, and of how many words I'd written. When I triumphantly produced the graphs to show progress to my publisher, she thought I was slightly mad.

Q: 'Is this a genuinely new idea or are you simply reworking a concept that's been around for years?'

A: Many of life's simple truths can be stated in different ways and can resonate with us differently at different times. Ancient wisdoms are often reworked in newer forms to suit contemporary circumstances and ideas.

In Chapter Two, we saw how psychology has evolved over recent years, such that the early objectivity of behaviourism has gradually shaded into the more subjective 'mindfulness' approach.

It may seem that, collectively, psychologists are simply revisiting a Buddhist truth known for thousands of years, but the context is very different at this point in time. It's like a big pendulum is slowly swinging, such that we revisit versions of previous approaches every 30 years or so. However, the ideas always seem to have a freshness and extra edge to them, mostly because of the technical and intellectual advances that have been made in the intervening years. You never swim in the same river twice.

Over the years, many books have invited us to find balance in our lives. In this book, we are yet again reminded to balance a present focus with a future focus. To balance active change with passive acceptance. To balance effortful achievement with sensory pleasure. These are not difficult concepts to understand, but in our increasingly complex lives, we just don't seem to be able to consistently apply them. To me, the Pleasure/Achievement Principle brings a very simple, unifying idea to our perennial search for balance and fulfilment in our lives, and brings that 'extra edge' that I mentioned earlier.

Q: 'Can the same activity be both a pleasure and an achievement?'

A: As I was writing this book, I found myself struggling to pull it all together. My publisher asked me if I was still *enjoying* writing it. It was a great question, because I'd become too preoccupied with achievement, and I'd lost sight of the pleasurable aspects of the activity.

Sure, it was a task with deadlines and clear outcomes, but writing was also a great pleasure. Remembering to enjoy my 'work' drew me back to what has, in the main, been a hugely indulgent pleasure! And as we have read, the way that you think about an activity largely determines how you perceive it.

Q: 'Is there a gender bias towards pleasure or achievement?'

A: This is yet to be studied. It would be tempting to suggest that men tend to be more driven and competitive, yet women probably express their achievement orientation in different ways. The busy housewife with the lazy husband would be one typical example that challenges that particular gender stereotype!

Either way, this book essentially focuses on you as an individual, whether male or female, and invites you to review your own lifestyle patterns, regardless of gender.

Appendix 1
THE PLEASURE/ACHIEVEMENT QUESTIONNAIRE

Use the following table to clarify your preference towards pleasure or achievement. The items are only examples of lifestyle decisions and do not necessarily reflect the overall influence of pleasure/achievement in your life. It serves as a general guide only.

	A	B	C		D	E	F
	Strongly agree	Agree	Mildly agree	I don't care	Mildly disagree	Disagree	Strongly disagree
After a meal, I prefer to sit down before I wash the dishes.	3	2	1	0	1	2	3
It is more important to me that my children are happy rather than that they do well.	3	2	1	0	1	2	3

When I look back on my life, I remember the fun that I've had, rather than the things that I've achieved.	3	2	1	0	1	2	3
On holiday, I prefer to relax on the beach rather than to explore places of local interest.	3	2	1	0	1	2	3
My friends tend to be fun to be with, rather than useful to know.	3	2	1	0	1	2	3
I try to be happy with myself as I am, rather than trying to change myself for the better.	3	2	1	0	1	2	3

I like to relax at the weekend, rather than getting things done.	3	2	1	0	1	2	3
I prefer spending money to making money.	3	2	1	0	1	2	3
During a break at work, I am more likely to snack rather than exercise.	3	2	1	0	1	2	3
I play sport for fun, rather than to win.	3	2	1	0	1	2	3

Your pleasure orientation

To estimate the strength of your pleasure orientation, add your scores from columns A, B and C. Write down your answer.

My total pleasure score:

0 to 5 = Weak

6 to 10 = Moderate

10 plus = Strong

Your achievement orientation

To estimate the strength of your achievement orientation, add your scores from columns D, E and F. Write down your answer.

My total achievement score:

0 to 5 = Weak

6 to 9 = Moderate

10 plus = Strong

Your overall engagement score

To obtain your overall engagement score, add your pleasure score to your achievement score. Write down your answer.

My engagement score:

0 to 10 = Low

11 to 20 = Medium

21 to 30 = High

Your overall pleasure/achievement bias

To obtain your overall pleasure/achievement bias, subtract your pleasure score from your achievement score. Write down your answer.

My values bias score:

A *negative* score indicates a mild, moderate or extremely *indulgent* lifestyle.

0 to −10 = Mild

−11 to −20 = Moderate

−21 to −30 = Extreme

A *positive* score indicates a mild, moderate or extremely *driven* lifestyle.

0 to 10 = Mild

11 to 20 = Moderate

21 to 30 = Extreme

My scores indicate that I am

mildly/moderately/extremely driven/indulgent.

(Circle the words that apply to your scores.)

Appendix 2
RELAXATION EXERCISES

Relaxation exercises provide us all with an easy technique to slow down and get in touch with an inner calmness. Used mainly as a technique for coping with stress, the exercises also offer a simple pathway to a quiet pleasurable state where we let go of ambition and focus instead on the moment.

The following four-part script is taken verbatim from my own Relaxation CD, in which I review the basic rationale for learning to relax, and talk clients through a series of simple instructions designed to induce a pleasurable state of calmness.

Introduction

Relaxation. Letting go of tension. Learning the skill and developing the ability to choose the degree of physical tension that we carry.

I would like to briefly consider some key concepts concerning muscle relaxation, and then move on to review a series of practical muscle tension and relaxation exercises that will help to promote a deep state of relaxation.

Our bodies are designed to tense up quickly. This ability has survival value and over the generations our ability to tense up quickly has allowed us to respond adaptively to danger or threat. It is the classic 'fight or flight' response, where by tensing our large muscle groups, we can fight or run away from threat or danger. Our large muscle groups tense up, our breathing becomes quicker, and our heart beats faster, pumping oxygenated blood to those large muscle groups.

At the same time, all non-essential functions close down. We stop digesting food or filing away memories in our cerebral cortex. Our perceptual awareness is significantly heightened. We lose peripheral vision as we focus intensely ahead, our eyes staring forward intently but darting from side to side in response to the slightest noise picked up by our acutely sensitive hearing. We are in a state of hypervigilance. It is 'all hands on deck' as we prepare to face danger.

Historically, these dangers have been physical dangers, but in contemporary society the threat is more psychological in nature. We worry about what people think of us, we worry about financial or emotional security, we worry about whether we will perform adequately or achieve to a self-imposed satisfactory standard. The degree to which we perceive the world as a threatening place is determined largely by our upbringing. There is a great deal of difference between individuals.

By scanning for potential threats we are inevitably creating a degree of physical tension in our body. A number of physical symptoms of stress may start to emerge, such as fine hand tremors, dryness in the throat, butterflies in the stomach or headaches. We may experience tingling sensations in our chest and arms or feel hot and flushed. In our state of heightened vigilance we find it harder to sleep, and this compounds our difficulties.

Other situations that generate muscle tension include chronic *pain* and environmental *stress*.

When we experience pain, our muscles will usually tense as a reflexive response. However, this muscle tension often compounds the tissue damage by introducing an extra strain at the site of the pain. We are tensing up when we need to relax.

In stressful environments, especially in the workplace, our response to the excessive demands made upon us, whether physical or psychological, lead to an increased degree of tension in our bodies. This often evolves slowly and we do not notice the accumulation of tensions that we take on board. We become irritable and tense, and our performance falls away as we become overwhelmed with the debilitating physical effects.

In general, people have little awareness of the degree of tension that they carry. As you look at people around you in the world, you will notice that some people seem relaxed and calm while others carry a degree of edgy alertness. Most of us naturally fall between the two extremes, but all of us have the ability to learn how to move from a state of tension to one of relaxation.

We can control our levels of tension. We can relax. In the next section we will look at a practical series of muscle tension and relaxation exercises designed to encourage a sense of physical calm.

Instructions for progressive muscle relaxation

I would like you to settle back and take some time to work through a practical series of exercises designed to promote relaxation. I would ask you to choose a time when you are not going to be interrupted, draw the curtains and switch off any artificial lights. It is best to lie on a bed or carpeted floor with a pillow under your head.

Have your arms by your sides and your hands with their palms facing downwards. Make sure the room is warm and loosen any tight-fitting clothing or jewellery. Give yourself every chance to relax and enjoy the experience of letting go.

We are going to work through the body in five different muscle groups, tensing and relaxing each group, building as we go. I shall ask you to tense up muscle groups tightly, then briefly hold that feeling of tension, and then relax. We are working our muscle fibres much as we would knead dough in making bread, flexing and warming our muscles to free them from tension.

Simply trying to relax from a standing start is rather difficult. However, by tensing up our muscles before trying to relax, we free them up to move, rather like taking a back swing in golf. By tensing up and then letting go, we allow our muscles to swing through to a state of relaxation like the pendulum of a clock. We tense up, we hold the tension, and we relax.

The first muscle group is the arms and hands. I would like you to bring up your arms and make tight fists, bending your elbows and holding your arms out to the sides. Hold it, feel the tension in your forearms and biceps, and relax. Let your arms slowly unfold to lie again, palms down, by your side. Notice that they are feeling a little bit warmer and a little bit heavier than before. This is the easiest part of your body to feel the relaxation response.

The second muscle group is your chest, back and neck. We will combine this with the previous exercise. I would like you to take a deep breath with your chest and as you breathe in, bring up your arms and make tight fists. Pull your shoulders back as if your shoulder blades are touching, push out your chest, push your head against the pillow. Feel the tension in your head, shoulders and neck, and relax. Let out a long sigh and let your arms unfold. Just notice that warm feeling spreading across your chest and back. Continue to take a few deep breaths with your chest, letting your chest rise and fall with a natural rhythm, like gentle waves on a beach, just rising and falling, very calm and very relaxed. Your body is feeling very warm, very calm, just slowing down and letting go.

The third muscle group is the tummy muscles. Again we will take a deep breath as our cue, breathing in, bringing up the arms and making tight fists, pulling your shoulders back, pushing your head against the pillow and then clench your tummy tight. Hold it, feel the tension in your tummy, then relax. Let your arms unfold and let out a long sigh. Again, taking nice deep breaths and letting go of the tension in your tummy. Allow that warm feeling to spread through your tummy, very calm, very relaxed, letting go of tension.

The fourth muscle group is your legs and feet. I want you to take a deep breath, bring up your arms, make tight fists, shoulders back, head against the pillow, clench your tummy tight, now push down hard with your heels and pull your toes up towards your head. Hold it, feel the tension in your thighs and calves, and relax. Then let out a long sigh, let your arms unfold, let go of all that tension in your legs and feet. It is as if your whole body is covered with a blanket, very warm, very heavy, very relaxed. Take nice deep breaths and enjoy that feeling of letting go.

The final muscle group is your head and face. There are lots of little muscles here and lots of instructions from me. Take a deep breath, bring up your arms, make tight fists, shoulders back, head against the pillow, clench your tummy tight, push down with your heels, pull your toes towards your head, now frown, screw up your eyes, wrinkle your nose, push your lips together, clench your jaw, push your tongue against the roof of your mouth, screw up your whole face really tight, hold it, feel the tension, and relax. Keeping your eyes closed, just let your arms unfold and let out a long sigh. Just take some deep breaths, be fully aware of the warmth and heaviness throughout your body. Just imagine a warm facecloth wiping across your forehead, wiping away the tension. No tension, no problems, being very relaxed, very calm, body feels great.

Relaxation ... It's a feeling that you can remember from your childhood. Just remember a time when you were young. Remember a place in the country where you could lie in the grass on a warm, sunny afternoon, looking into the sky, feeling a warm gentle breeze across your forehead. Smell the freshness and feel the earth beneath you. The sounds of traffic and other children playing seem far away. You have a lot of space and a lot of time. Gaze up into the blue sky. Just watch the clouds drifting past, very calm, very relaxed. Breathing very calming you feel completely at peace with the world around you. With each breath you take you become more and more relaxed.

This is a very special feeling that you can always carry with you.

Relaxing in imagination

As you lie in a state of relaxation, you can take the time to remember similar experiences that may come to mind. Imagine that you are looking at a *white candle* glowing with a steady yellow flame in a darkened room. Gaze deeply into the yellow flame, it may flicker occasionally but continue to gaze at the constant warm glow that comes from the centre of the flame. Allow the candle to glow steadily and in your mind connect with the calmness within the flame.

Move on to picture the image of a *red rose* in full bloom. Imagine that you lean into the rose and smell a sweet fragrance. As you breathe in, your head fills with the sensation of colour and perfume. With each breath you feel more relaxed and more peaceful. You feel the muscles in your face relax as the tension flows away. Feel the warmth radiate throughout your body.

Finally, I would like you to imagine that you are *lying on the beach* on a warm, sunny afternoon with sounds of children playing far away and the waves gently rising and falling with a natural rhythm. Allow your breathing to fall into the same rhythm as the sea. Watch the waves roll in, rise, break gently, dissolve into the sand before drawing back out to the sea. Your chest rises and then falls with a natural rhythm. Just hold your breath slightly after you have inhaled and enjoy that moment of perfection before you breathe out.

Your breathing has a natural cycle and as you slow your breathing down you will become more and more relaxed. Just take a few more breaths before you finish. Scan through your body once more, slowing right down, letting go, feeling very calm, very relaxed. It's a very special feeling that you can always carry with you.

Now open your eyes and just lie for a few moments. You will be getting up slowly to move calmly through the next part of your day. Alternatively, continue to lie where you are, perhaps listen to some music, and relax.

Brief imaginal relaxation

Once you have mastered the skill of progressive muscle relaxation, it is useful to learn a brief *imaginal* version that allows you to quickly talk yourself down into a calm, relaxed state. You can use this prior to an important appointment, in dentists' waiting rooms, in lifts, in supermarket queues or in aeroplanes. In any situation where you find that you tense up, you can use brief imaginal relaxation to talk yourself down.

Start by putting your hands in your lap, one hand on top of the other. Cast your eyes downwards, perhaps to where the leg of a chair or table meets the floor. Now focus your thoughts on your hands and notice the warmth between them. Imagine that your hands are becoming so warm and so heavy that you can't lift them.

Take deep breaths and imagine with each breath you are drawing the warmth up your arms and across your chest, a steady glow of warmth being drawn through your body. Keep taking nice, deep, steady breaths, your chest rising and falling with a natural rhythm like gentle waves on a beach. Let that warm feeling spread down through your tummy and into your legs.

Notice the nice warm feeling. It feels as if you are covered with a blanket, very calm, very heavy, very relaxed. Imagine a warm facecloth wiping across your forehead, wiping away the tension. No tension, no problems. Slowing down and letting go. You are feeling very calm, very relaxed. Your body is glowing with a sense of calmness. Regardless of the turbulent world around you, you can move forward calmly and serenely. You can control your level of tension, you can relax.

·

I hope that you have enjoyed these exercises and that the techniques I have described allow you to take more control of the physical levels of tension in your body. You can choose to feel more confident in yourself, and to respond positively to the often challenging demands of a busy life. By learning to relax, we learn to enjoy life more and give ourselves the opportunity to achieve to our fullest potential. I wish you the very best for your future.

If you would like to download the spoken version of this relaxation script, please visit my website at www.chrisskellettconsulting.co.nz.

FURTHER READING

Books about general happiness

Happiness: The Science Behind Your Smile, Daniel Nettle, 2005, Oxford University Press, New York.

The Happiness Hypothesis: Finding Modern Truth in Ancient Wisdom, Jonathan Haidt, 2006, Basic Books, New York.

Stumbling on Happiness: Think You Know What Makes You Happy?, Daniel Gilbert, 2006, Alfred A. Knopf, New York.

Books with a 'Pleasure' focus

The Power of Now: A Guide to Spiritual Enlightenment, Eckhart Tolle, 1999, Namaste Publishing, Vancouver, Canada.

Choosing Happiness: Short Answers to the Big Questions, Stephanie Dowrick and Catherine Greer, 2005, Allen and Unwin, Sydney.

Openness, Clarity, Sensitivity, Michael Hookham, 1992, Longchen Foundation, Oxford, UK.

The Art of Happiness, His Holiness the Dalai Lama and Howard C. Cutler MD, 1998, Riverhead Books, New York.

Happier, Tal Ben-Shahar PhD, 2007, McGraw-Hill, New York.

Books with an 'Achievement' focus

The 7 Habits of Highly Effective People: Powerful Lessons in Personal Change, Stephen R. Covey, 1989, Free Press, New York.

The Purpose Driven Life: What on Earth am I Here For?, Rick Warren, 2002, Zondervan Books, Grand Rapids, Michigan.

The Winner's Bible: Rewire Your Brain for Permanent Change, Dr Kerry Spackman, 2009, The Winner's Institute, Atlanta, Georgia.

Make Success Your Friend: One Hundred and One Practical Tips for What Succeeds, Tim Sole, 2004, Random House, New York.

From Good to Great: Why Some Companies Make the Leap, and Others Don't, Jim Collins, 2001, Harper Collins, New York.

Unlimited Power: The New Science of Personal Achievement, Anthony Robbins, 2003, Free Press, New York.

Books about clinical psychology

Cognitive Therapy and the Emotional Disorders, Aaron T. Beck, 1976, International Universities Press, New York.

Reinventing Your Life: The Breakthrough Program to End Negative Behavior and Feel Great Again, Jeffrey E. Young PhD and Janet Klosko PhD, 1994, Plume Books, New York.

Get Out of Your Mind and Into Your Life: The New Acceptance and Commitment Therapy, Steven C. Hayes and Spencer Smith, 2005, New Harbinger Publications, Oakland, California.

Authentic Happiness: Using the New Positive Psychology to Realize Your Potential for Lasting Fulfillment, Martin E.P. Seligman, PhD, 2002, Free Press, New York.

The Happiness Trap: Stop Struggling, Start Living, Dr Russ Harris, 2007, Exisle Publishing, NSW, Australia.

Useful websites

www.authentichappiness.org

www.worlddatabaseofhappiness.eur.nl

www.happiness-project.com

www.thehappinessshow.com

Acknowledgements

To my wonderfully tolerant wife, Lois, whose unrelenting lists of 'things to do' provide a perfect balance for my chronic tendency towards televised sport. And to our children, Lucy, Jessica and Henry, whose good humour brings so much Pleasure to our lives, and whose Achievements bring us so much pride.

Also, to the team at Exisle Publishing, who are a wonderful family to be a part of, and especially Anouska Jones, my editor. I would also like to thank Barbara Larson and Nick Wright for their work on an earlier draft of the manuscript, and Geoff Norman, whose belief in the overall concept kept me going through my darkest hour!

Finally, to all those friends and clients whose anecdotes and simple inspirational truths have added so much substance to this book, it was my conversations with you that sparked the initial development of the Pleasure/Achievement concept, and it is now your stories that make it all feel so very real.

Index

ALSO FROM EXISLE PUBLISHING …

The 1000 Most Important Questions You Will Ever Ask Yourself
Alyss Thomas

A world-wide success story, this self-help classic is now available in a new edition.

Experienced psychotherapist Alyss Thomas has closely observed what goes wrong in people's lives and, by applying the principles of psychology in a positive way, she provides you with the tools to achieve the outcomes you really desire.

Each section of the book is laid out in a clear quiz format, to give you your own complete workout in such key areas of life as your personal values, anxiety, stress, time, confidence, self-esteem, relaxation, dealing with the past, depression, loss, grief, joy, creativity and happiness.

You'll find that you will refer to this book again and again. Fun to use and easy to read, it's for everyone who wants a happy fulfilled life!

ISBN 978 1 921497 32 2

Release Your Worries

Dr Cate Howell & Dr Michele Murphy

The most enjoyable book you will ever read about dealing with stress and anxiety!

Written by experts, Release Your Worries is just the tool you need to help you take control of your anxieties. The authors understand that what works for one person may not work for another. This is why they have drawn on simple yet effective techniques from a range of the most up-to-date psychological approaches, including:

- Cognitive Behavioural Therapy
- Narrative Therapy
- Relaxation Therapy and Hypnotherapy
- Acceptance and Commitment Therapy (ACT)
- Constructive Living, and
- Mindfulness-based strategies.

Case studies illustrate key points, while exercises are included to guide you on the path to nurturing mind, body and spirit. With its clear, down-to-earth approach, *Release Your Worries* will enable you to start making a positive difference in your life immediately.

ISBN 978 1 921497 43 8